POETRY REV

WINTER 1996/97 VOLUME
EDITOR PETER FORBES
ASSISTANT EDITOR MARTIN DR
SUBSCRIPTIONS AND ADVERTISING SOF

CONTENTS

Modern Poetry in Translation

Autumn 1996 : No 10 -Russian Poetry

More than 30 poets + feature on Joseph Brodsky

Still available : No 3 - Polish poets,
including **Nobel Prize laureate Wisława Szymborska**,
Anna Kamieńska and others + *Italy, France*

and

1: Bonnefoy + *Pasolini, Cassou, Celan and others*
2: Franz Baermann Steiner (*trans. by Michael Hamburger*)
4: Jerusalem International Poets Festival (1993): *34 poets*
5: Galician Troubadours + *Pessoa, Cernuda, Heine + others*
6: Brazil: *19 Brazilian poets + others*
7: Wales: *18 poets + essays, reviews*
8: France: *13 French poets, lipograms, essays + other Europeans*
9: East and West: *Filipino + Asian and European poets*

Coming in 1997:

11 : Peruvian poets and others; featured translator: James Kirkup
12 : Dutch and Flemish poetry

Single issues (200-240 pages) -   **£9.50 (UK and rest of EU) post free**
                 $18 (overseas) post free
- or try your local bookshop !

Subscriptions (2 issues per annum) - pro rata

Details and sample copies from:
Norma Rinsler, MPT, King's College London,
Strand, London WC2R 2LS, UK

Cheques (payable to King's College London)
should be sent to **Norma Rinsler**

Funded by
THE
ARTS
COUNCIL
OF ENGLAND

POETRY REVIEW
SUBSCRIPTIONS
Four issues including postage:

UK individuals £23
Overseas individuals £31
(all overseas delivery is by airmail)
USA individuals $56

Libraries, schools and institutions:
UK £30
Overseas £37
USA $66

Single issue £5.95 + 50p p&p (UK)

Sterling and US dollar payments only.
Eurocheques, Visa and Mastercard
payments are acceptable.

Bookshop distribution:
Password Books
Telephone 0161 953 4009

Design by Philip Lewis

Typeset by Poetry Review

Printed by Warwick Printing Co Ltd at
Theatre Street, Warwick CV34 4DR
and at 112 Bermondsey Street,
London SE1 3TX
Telephone 0171 378 1579

POETRY REVIEW is the magazine of
the Poetry Society. It is published
quarterly and issued free to members
of the Poetry Society. Poetry Review
considers submissions from non-
members and members alike. To
ensure reply submissions must be
accompanied by an SAE or adequate
International Reply coupons: Poetry
Review accepts no responsibility for
contributions that are not reply paid.

Founded 24 February 1909
Charity Commissioners No: 303334
© 1996

EDITORIAL AND BUSINESS ADDRESS:
22 BETTERTON STREET, LONDON WC2H 9BU

telephone   **0171 240 4810**
fax   **0171 240 4818**
email   **poetrysoc@dial.pipex.com**

THE POETRY SOCIETY

ISBN 1 900771 03 9
ISSN 0032 2156

Funded by
THE
ARTS
COUNCIL
OF ENGLAND

BEYOND THE BELL JAR

by Peter Forbes

AS CAROL RUMENS points out in her review of Maura Dooley's anthology *Making for Planet Alice* (p. 26), there has been a plethora of women's anthologies in recent years. Not quite the good thing it might seem, according to the editor of the '80s anthology *Making for the Open*. Rumens makes the case against "women's poetry": that it sells so well as a genre item, the male-dominated canon is left unchanged, and that the books are never edited, reviewed or read by men. I hope this issue will be seen in a different light.

One might wonder at the severity of Rumens' judgement until you read one of Dennis O'Driscoll's cullings from his *Poetry Ireland Review* column, Pickings and Choosings, collected in the bumper 50th issue (summer 1996), edited by Michael Longley. O'Driscoll caught Derek Mahon, in the *Irish Times*, saying the following:

> Must it be said that, for all the trumpeting about women poets, the empress has no clothes? That she is a Lady Godiva after all?

You don't often meet such totally unreconstructed males these days, but presumably he was only saying what many male poets mutter into their beer. The same case is put with more wit by Jason Strugnell on page 77 of this issue. We think, *pace* Mahon and Strugnell, that this issue can demonstrate a nifty range of female poetic raiment, and that it is tending to relegate the trousers to the back of the store.

A consequence of the New Generation Poets promotion known only to the editor of this magazine is that, for all its virtues, it disrupted our programme of featuring, every two to three years, poets who had not yet published a book. New Generation was an attempt to bring to a wider audience poets who often had several books behind them. Our last New Poets special was Autumn 1992, which included Susan Wicks, W. N. Herbert and Sophie Hannah. Having produced New Generation in Spring 1994 we could hardly launch into another New Poets issue soon after. Since Spring 1996 we have featured new poets in every issue (the series continues with Jane Holland in this issue – p. 49). But there is a missing generation: poets who published first books in the last four years and are now winning prizes.

There is every sign that this is a very good generation, but what is special about it is that almost anybody's list of the new poets will consist of about 75 per cent women. Seven out of the last nine Forward First Collection prize shortlist have been women. I decided that the main feature in this issue would include only women: unfair to the new male poets, as New Generation was unfair to the just-over-40s, but to have featured two or three token men alongside the women would have weakened the theme.

And the theme isn't artificial. This is the first time that a new crop of poets has been predominantly female. There is no dominant style, although the rise of formalism is noteworthy, especially of the light verse kind practised by Sophie Hannah and Eleanor Brown. We sent the featured poets a questionnaire, and, besides much else of interest, the most frequently cited influence, inspiration and rôle model for the poets is Carol Ann Duffy. Her *Anvil New Poets* anthology launched poets like Alice Oswald and Kate Clanchy, and her exemplary career ought to make even Mahon sit up.

When we began this issue, we heard that Bloodaxe were rushing out *Making for Planet Alice*. There are 30 poets in Maura Dooley's anthology, 11 in the *Review*. *Alice* contains several well established poets, several of whom were featured in New Generation Poets. With our very different publishing history, we decided not to feature any of the New Generation poets – these are post-New Generation poets with one collection apiece (except for the prolific Sophie Hannah who's already on her second book). I hope that this issue – edited by a man, many of the reviews of women by men – will answer some of Carol Rumens' objections to the way in which women's poetry is handled.

Unlike anthologies, mainstream magazines cannot address themselves exclusively to a niche. We have only four issues a year and they sell roughly the same quantities irrespective of the contents, over 90 per cent being sold on advance subscription. Which is to say: this is not a marketing exercise – it is the state of play at the beginning of 1997.

ELEANOR BROWN

THE WAY INTO POETRY: "It falls in spirals / to land upon my free hand / tired, with trembling wings".

HEROINES AND HEROES: "I come to admire / Anon who has the good taste / to remain anon".

INFLUENTIAL CONTEMPORARIES: "Which of the bright leaves / the naked tree once fluttered / seems to it most lost?".

READINGS: "I've readings enough. / Let me give readings to all / those who lack readings".

KEEPING UP: "Innocence preserved / by the chill of ignorance / loses its fresh scent".

NEW POPULISM: "Hurt men bring water / in cupped hands to the dying. / One exclaims 'The waste!'".

NEW GENERATION POETS: "You pass me by. So. / If you never come again, / I never know you".

THE WOMAN QUESTION: "There are good women. / Poets publish poetry. / Why do you think this?".

7 OUT OF 9 RECENT FORWARD FIRST COLLECTION WINNERS HAVE BEEN WOMEN: "Seven out of nine; / seventy seven per cent; / now draw a pie chart".

KEEPING THE DAY JOB? "Fierce night poetry / careering out of control – / hang on to the day.".

FURTHER COMMENTS: "The Questionary / is an ugly beast, best kept / by statisticians".

COLLECTION: *Maiden Speech* (Bloodaxe, £6.95).

ONE FOR KEATS AND ONE FOR ME

I

I had caviar once.
Real, red caviar,
gleaming like jellied rubies
cast at the feet of a Tsar;
winking in flickering candlelight,
piled on a silver fork,
colour of blood, colour of song,
salt grapes without a stalk.

Stroking the tongue with a sea-breeze,
mouthful of yielding pearls
charged with a cool explosive,
caviar unfurls
fresh fish brine on the palate,
a fallout of delight
from a bursting of poppy-petals,
a silent Fireworks Night.

II

Sainsburys Pickled Silverskins
don't taste like caviar
vinegared baby onions
is really all they are
but they pop quite well on the roof of your mouth
and they're only a quid a jar.

BAD TASTE

You're losing it. You're letting yourself go;
your home's a dump, your neighbours are all rotten –
they set a bad example. You've forgotten
your duties as a host. Now, say hello.

I'll ask you how you are. Tell pleasant lies:
remember, this is how it's done. To mention
the folly of the question draws attention
to the mendacity of the replies.

Because – if you want honesty – I think
I liked you better when you were still living;
to tell the truth, however unforgiving
it sounds, I can't help noticing you stink.

I liked you more before your bones poked through
your flesh (which wasn't green); when your eye-sockets
were less like craters left by two gone rockets;
in short, I liked you more when you were you.

Old possum, don't just lie there playing dead,
as though my visit were an interruption.
Are you so busy studying corruption
you can't sit up and answer me instead?

Tell me I write a lousy elegy.
Tell me that this is all in dreadful taste.
Tell me: what's more obscene than fucking waste?
Death is in quite poor taste, if you ask me.

TESSA ROSE CHESTER

THE WAY INTO POETRY: "It's around us from the beginning, in nursery rhymes, chants, songs – it's up to us to hear it. For me, writing poetry was as natural as drawing or playing the piano, and was encouraged by my parents and school".

HEROINES AND HEROES: "At different times – Hopkins, Dylan Thomas, Shakespeare, Plath, Eliot, Lorca".

INFLUENTIAL CONTEMPORARIES: "Probably Duffy, Hughes, Heaney, Holub, Shuttle, Szirtes; definitely Dave Smith, Peter Redgrove, and possibly others".

KEEPING UP: Reads *PN Review, Poetry Review, The Rialto, Stand, Writing Women* "and any others I find".

NEW POPULISM: "Anything that demystifies it as some sacred art, and makes people see it as something living, relevant, beautiful, powerful, immediate, is to be encouraged".

NEW GENERATION POETS: "It brought names to my attention I was unaware of before; the hype was fun, though I felt sorry for those not selected. It raised poetry's profile for a while, which must be good".

KEEPING THE DAY JOB? "I wish a career in poetry was a realistic proposition. But I have a mortgage and bills like everyone else".

COLLECTION: *Provisions of Light* (Oxford Poets, £6.99).

THE WAR

The war is imminent. It hasn't quite
begun. We search in vain for cellars, dank
depressing basements, orderly, polite.
We line the subways. Every face is blank;
works by Henry Moore in sketch and stone.
Considering what it means to die alone.

The war will come. The radios are dead,
the streets are full of dust from shuffling feet.
I'm in a queue of one, one, one. I head
my own detachment; ordered to retreat
I cower in the gutter, whittling bone.
Defining how it looks to die alone.

This war will end all wars. And I am dumb
with terror at the loss of everything
I know. You are never with me, in some
other place or on another plane
and I have minutes to not reach the phone.
Disputing why I have to die alone

And now the fires sweep round the hill.
We stay blind. Pathetic. Still.

COMING OF AGE: JULY 1933

Her room absorbs the lustre
of a summer night.

In slowly pearling sheets
the dress from Berwick Street

lingers
like a wet dark dream.

Her first black dress.
Pantherine. Dangerous.

She slips it on,
frilling out the short lace sleeves.

Wrapped tight round her throat
it plunges down her back

in ribbons of ebony.
Mother won't approve

that knowing curve.
All that white flesh.

It dances by itself
in front of the mirror.

She is a gift-wrapped lily
slender as a ghost,

anticipating how each breath
will shimmer up her spine

and set the velvet folds
murmuring.

***

The photographer is charmed,
taking twice as long to fix the lights.

Punctual, holds herself well.
She has a natural grace

if rather camera-shy:
a perfect focus for my new display.

Later
he colours-up the print,

bringing out the blue
in the cloudy eyes,

the chestnut tones
in soft waved hair.

A hint of red
on lips and cheek

and she's in the window
labelled OUR BANSTEAD BELLE,

admired by all
until her mother passes by

and has the photograph removed.
Being twenty-one

bought no freedom then:
only a dress

worn like a shadow
sewn into her skin.

KATE CLANCHY

THE WAY INTO POETRY: "I started writing as a result of reading Carol Ann Duffy, and continued because of her encouragement on an Arvon course".

HEROINES AND HEROES: Donne, Marvell, Yeats, Larkin, MacNeice, Simon Armitage, Don Paterson, Michael Donaghy.

INFLUENTIAL CONTEMPORARIES: Carol Ann Duffy, Selima Hill.

KEEPING UP: Reads *London Review of Books, Poetry Review, TLS*, reviews for *The Independent* and *The Scotsman.*

NEW POPULISM: "What's to disapprove of? Outside of the literary world, this 'populism' still isn't very popular".

NEW GENERATION POETS: Positive.

THE WOMAN QUESTION: "I think a generation of appropriately educated women are reaching an appropriate age. This may sound bland but it's an amazing position to be in".

7 OUT OF 9 RECENT FORWARD FIRST COLLECTION WINNERS HAVE BEEN WOMEN: "I think this statistic is probably coincidence or some orgasmic heave of the Zeitgeist".

KEEPING THE DAY JOB? "I am going freelance – but as a writer, not just a poet".

COLLECTION: *Slattern* (Chatto, £6.99).

WAR POETRY

The class have dropped their books. The janitor's
disturbed some wasps, broomed the nest
straight off the roof. It lies outside, exotic
as a fallen planet, a burst city of the poor;
its newsprint halls, its ashen, tiny rooms
all open to the air. The insects' buzz
is low-key as a smart machine. They form,
re-form, in stacks and coils, advance
and cross like pulsing points on radar screens.

And of these boys who shave their heads
wear football strips, who would, they swear,
enlist at once, shoot conchies down,
not one runs out, hands clasped on head,
to bag the queen or pike the nest,
to lap the yard with grapeshot face,
brandishing that squat grey head.
They watch the wasps through glass,
silently, abashed, the way we all watch war.

ON THE BRIDGE OVER THE BORDER

Here, I should surely think of home –
my country and the neat steep town
where I grew up: its banks of cloud,
its winds and changing, stagey light,
its surly, horizontal rain, or failing that,

the time the train stuck here for half an hour.
It was hot, for once. The engine seemed
to grunt and breathe with us,
and in the hush, the busker at the back
struck up *Scotland the Brave*. There was

a filmic, golden light and the man opposite
was struck, he said, with love for me.
He saw something in my eyes. But
he was from Los Angeles, and I, in any case,
was thinking of another bridge. It was

October. I was running to meet a man
with whom things were not quite settled,
were not, in fact, to ever settle, and I stopped
halfway to gaze at birds – swallows
in their distant thousands, bound

for Africa, or heat, or home, not knowing
which, but certain how. Shifting on the paper sky,
they were crosses on a changing graph,
they were sand in a hoop shaken sideways,
and I stared as if panning for gold.

JULIA COPUS

THE WAY INTO POETRY: "Via Sylvia Plath's *The Bell Jar*, which I read early in '92. The book intrigued me so much that I got a biography on Plath out of the library, which, of course, quoted extracts from her poems. When I read the *Collected Poems* the poetry excited me in a way I had not experienced before ... [it] seemed so urgent and so absolutely genuine that I was left with a strange mixture of admiration and envy: to be able to express oneself in that way must, I thought, be the greatest feeling imaginable".

HEROINES AND HEROES: Chaucer ("for his humanity and humour"), Elizabeth Bishop, Pablo Neruda, Plath.

INFLUENTIAL CONTEMPORARIES: "I am as much influenced by novels, films and music as poetry".

KEEPING UP: Reads *London Magazine, The North, Poetry Review, The Rialto*.

NEW POPULISM: "To refer to David Kennedy's point on new populism, in the last issue of *Poetry Review*: if an exhibition of Pamela Anderson posters is going to draw people into the National Gallery (I wonder, incidentally, how many women it would attract) all well and good. So long as those people come back to see what else is on offer. There is something a bit tacky about the new populism – if Rudyard Kipling's 'If' is a measure of its efficacy perhaps it's time to move on".

NEW GENERATION POETS: "Anything that increases the readership for poetry has to be a good thing. On the other hand, lists like this are always arbitrary to a degree, and the criteria for the New Gen Poets promotion in particular perhaps resulted in a rather misleading representation of the best 'new' poets around".

THE WOMAN QUESTION: "Women poets publishing today are second generation, so to speak. This means not only that the hardest part of the fight has been won for us, but that we have rôle models where our rôle models had none".

7 OUT OF 9 RECENT FORWARD FIRST COLLECTION WINNERS HAVE BEEN WOMEN: "The Forward awards are not the only prizes to reveal this trend: last year's finalists in the Poetry Business's pamphlet competition, for example, were all women. The cause is hard to identify, but I think the poetry scene is a microcosm of what's going on generally in the West at the moment".

KEEPING THE DAY JOB? "There *are* opportunities around for writing-based jobs. I think a lot of travelling and organising is time- and energy-consuming, and can detract from the real job of writing. Perhaps Kafka and Larkin had the right idea after all ...".

COLLECTION: *The Shuttered Eye* (Bloodaxe, £6.95).

DESKSCAPE

The surface is cracked in places, long cracks like the parched
mud of a river-bed, with its silt of flakes and dirt,
old abandoned thoughts. In the window the sixty watt

bulb thinks it is a moon, shining like a saint from its hood
of metal. Blameless; it asks for nothing. In reality
it is a meddler and a snoop, craning its rubber

neck over the paper to catch the words it knows will
fall soon helter-skelter with the dust. It likes to watch
them half-formed and struggling for a shape. Bright lidless eye –

What does it care if they survive or not? So I keep them,
for a long time, tucked like secrets in the sleeve of my mouth.
There are too many distractions here. Even the flowers

torment me. I push my thumbnail into them and their
plump flesh darkens and weeps round the little wound.
And they will go on weeping far into the night;

weeping and breathing loudly in their fat jug, putrefying
in the dark. They do not need me; without me this whole
house would exist quite happily; the staircase would go on

guiding the carpet up to the same room, the exact same
desk with its small planet, its beautiful wildlife.
I am under no illusions: I would not be missed.

KAFKA'S PAPERS

It is the dry season: words
unwritten, thoughts stacked up
like hay. Today he burned

the first thin leaves of his manuscripts;
the flames tensed for each pale offering.
In bed he becomes absorbed by the light

weight of wrists at the end of his arms,
which he crosses now over his chest – a soldier
with his pack. Sleep, he is thinking:

the unconquerable land.
Tomorrow he will try again
to write himself into the depths

of the paper. Dry paper. He will pour
himself into it. He thinks of the fire
that will free him finally; a secret

kept like a touchpaper between friends –
This is how his life was, Max will say:
all the colours and moods, the fierce

embers and the supple flames, ochre
and pale violet, their hunger, their endless
reaching up, and the white ash flying

like moths; the inevitable fading,
low-rolling smokes – everything
he wrote was like this,

as passionate, as mortal.

JANE DURAN

THE WAY INTO POETRY: "The high school I went to in New York City encouraged creativity and my English teachers gave me a grounding in poetry and the use of traditional verse forms. My mother wrote poems herself and I learned a lot about the craft from her. At university I took creative writing courses and began to focus on free verse. I moved to England in 1966, joined Dinah Livingstone's ILEA class, in 1986 and started writing in earnest".

HEROINES AND HEROES: William Blake, T. S. Eliot, William Carlos Williams, Federico García Lorca, George Seferis, C. P. Cavafy, Pablo Neruda, Elizabeth Bishop and Rainer Maria Rilke. There are many, many others too.

INFLUENTIAL CONTEMPORARIES: Allen Ginsberg, Sylvia Plath, Elizabeth Bishop, Sharon Olds.

KEEPING UP: Reads *The American Poetry Review, The North, PN Review, Poetry London Newsletter, Poetry Review, The Rialto, TLS*.

NEW POPULISM: "National Poetry Day is a lovely idea and I'm all for it – readings in Covent Garden, poetry activities in schools and libraries … Poetry should certainly be for everyone, because it is about us all, but that doesn't mean standards need to be compromised. It should still be real poetry".

THE WOMAN QUESTION: "I think this probably mirrors representation in other walks of life. Women are being heard more, but the balance of power is still with men".

KEEPING THE DAY JOB? "To make an actual living from poetry I imagine you need to be either very famous or have a regular job such as teaching creative writing at a university or working as a poetry editor".

COLLECTION: *Breathe Now, Breathe* (Enitharmon, £5.95).

COASTAL

I love your old age,
days when you repeat stories
and the screen door opens
into the parlour of your kitchen.
Your neighbours are without
salt or sugar, wanting to come in
in their tucked-in dresses,
their mops put by,

those tribal processions –
baldness of husbands, sons,
bearded mothers. Fish scaled
and left in the smokehouse,
the sea losing its haze.

They leave behind conversations,
silences, old rope for new.
Your stories tether back
to those first porches.
Who can sleep in the summer months
under such patchwork –
the heat of the past,
the lighthouse room?

The seals have grown old
here too, in the worn-out
quilts of the sea, gusts.
We breathe the same air.
Some nights they look in at us
from the galleries of their whiskers,
streaked with salt, with mating.

I know each moment –
stories that wash up,
coasts that take and take the light,
the first beaten-back mornings.

ELVIS

When the record arrived from New York –
over the Panama Canal, down the coast
near Buenaventura past rotting fruit
you could discern and through Antofagasta
which is one hot breath for a desert rose
and into the cool precincts of Santiago

with its stirred cherry trees and magnolias,
they came right over: flat-chested Lorna,
Irene with the freckled bare feet
that smelled of grass, Rosi
with the muscular legs and long lashes,
Gabriela innocent and smiling

who always arrived late.
We danced to the songs, practising.
We got so good. The song was Anyplace
is Paradise (when I'm with you).
At the time I was reading Wuthering Heights.
That room held me. The mauve-striped shirt

on the record sleeve, the cherry trees
fighting with each other for light
in our garden, for an actual glimpse
over the wall. I would play Anyplace
is Paradise and read Wuthering Heights.
I would play Anyplace is Paradise

and Heathcliff bowed to kiss her
feverishly. Heathcliff in the stable.
Heathcliff weeping. The mauve shirt.
I could see the snow-capped mountains
from my window. The huaso tunes,
the excitement of the nearby huasos

climbing the slopes on their ponies,
dead ringers for Heathcliff,
the boys from The Grange, Elvis.
Anyplace. Anyplace is.

SOPHIE HANNAH

THE WAY INTO POETRY: "Through reading it as a child, writing it a lot at primary school, doing a Creative Writing course at Manchester University".

HEROINES AND HEROES: P. B. Shelley, W. B. Yeats, E. E. Cummings, Robert Frost, Edna St Vincent Millay, C. H. Sisson, James Fenton.

INFLUENTIAL CONTEMPORARIES: Wendy Cope, Glyn Maxwell.

KEEPING UP: Reads and reviews for *PN Review, Poetry Review*; reads *TLS*.

NEW POPULISM: "I approve in theory, but not always of the winners – if you could ensure that the best people won, I'd approve totally".

NEW GENERATION POETS: "As above – a good idea, but some of the poets chosen I thought were dubious choices".

THE WOMAN QUESTION: "I think there are fewer really good poets than people make out, of either gender".

7 OUT OF 9 RECENT FORWARD FIRST COLLECTION WINNERS HAVE BEEN WOMEN: "Perhaps more women entered than men? Or else a coincidence. I don't believe women are intrinsically better poets than men".

KEEPING THE DAY JOB? "It can be realistic to have a career in poetry, if you do enough readings and teaching, but I believe in hanging onto the day job anyway because (a) it keeps you in touch with the real world as well as the world of writing and writers, (b) if you have another job, writing seems more like fun and less like work".

COLLECTIONS: *The Hero and the Girl Next Door* (Carcanet, £6.95); *Hotels, like Houses* (Carcanet, £6.95) – reviewed on p. 62.

THE YELLOW AND THE BLUE

Could be an armband or a rubber ring,
a lilo or a surfboard or a boat,
a wave (it needn't be a man-made thing)
that makes it briefly possible to float;
could be the lotion I slap on, rub in
to give the sun the temper of the shade,
or the umbrella that relieves my skin
while others turn to leather and to suede;
could be that in the pool or on the beach,
could be that in the yellow and the blue,
the tourist's miracles within my reach
are not commissioned or inspired by you,
and if to me you're block, board, ring and band
I am, as much as this is not, your land.

THIS MORNING IN A BLACK JAG

In this ringroad-and-roundabout business park of a place,
Where the favourite phrases are modem and user-base
And a poet is probably seen as a waste of space,
I'm in need of a mode of transport and a familiar face

And I seem to have picked up a car with a man that drives –
Whenever I order a cab, it is he who arrives,
Drops me off at my nines and collects me from my fives,
And although for the bulk of the days we lead totally separate lives,

When I mentioned some places up north, he knew where they were,
And he even conceded Oasis were better than Blur,
And Jim Morrison blares from his cab, though he says he'd prefer
To be thought of not as a taxi driver but as a chauffeur.

To prove it, he turned up this morning in a black Jag,
And, while teaching bored youths how to write is no less of a drag
(You're explaining the sonnet, they're planning which lessons to wag),
It's more bearable when you turn up in a car about which you can brag.

Stroppy kids can't depress me – I'm lucky enough to have found
A man who leaves every day free just to drive me around,
Who asks how it went and who tells me which schools are renowned
For reducing the squeamish to tears. We have covered a fair bit of ground

And we secretly wonder (we're both too polite to enquire)
Why his fares are much lower these days, why my tips are much higher,
Why our journeys get longer each time, so we tend to go via
This diversion or that, both pretending there's scenery there to admire.

For our last trip, he charges me half the original quote:
Just two pounds, but he gets the change from my five pound note
And I get the smell of his Jaguar on my coat
And a train journey home to read and re-read the receipts he wrote.

GWYNETH LEWIS

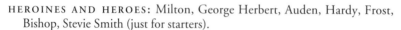

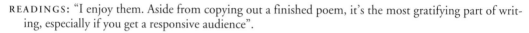

THE WAY INTO POETRY: "Out of the blue I started to write an epic poem on the rain when I was seven. It took me all of one Easter holiday. I wrote a lot in school, had two pamphlets published, but later hit a block in university. Since then I've been trying to get back to the pure contentment and delight of that first poem – me sitting at a table trying to describe the world in rhyme".

HEROINES AND HEROES: Milton, George Herbert, Auden, Hardy, Frost, Bishop, Stevie Smith (just for starters).

INFLUENTIAL CONTEMPORARIES: Les Murray, C. K. Williams, Joseph Brodsky.

READINGS: "I enjoy them. Aside from copying out a finished poem, it's the most gratifying part of writing, especially if you get a responsive audience".

KEEPING UP: *Poetry Review, TLS, Verse,* Welsh periodicals, the Sunday supplements, and magazines in the USA; reviews for *Poetry Review,* but prefers to write more general articles on poetry.

THE NEW POPULISM: "I approve. The more we hear about poetry the better. I don't think it does at all to be snooty about the kind of poetry being promoted. The uses of poetry are many and it's not for any one group of people to decide what people should like . . . I do believe that people respond to the best in all areas – see, for example, Auden's poem in *Four Weddings and a Funeral,* which people liked very much when it wasn't presented as 'poetry'".

NEW GENERATION POETS: "Negative in that I wasn't in it (even though I didn't qualify!) but positive in that it raised the profiles of a whole lot of good writers. This could only do the rest of us and the cause of poetry in general good".

THE WOMAN QUESTION: "This generation of women is reaping the benefits of previous feminist campaigns. Perhaps more women have the 'head-space' needed to write well – and there are more responsive listeners to those voices among editors. I also like a good deal of the poetry coming from men at the moment, which suggests changes of a wider nature than simply issues of gender have taken place".

KEEPING THE DAY JOB? "I think it's perfectly possible to have a career in poetry today. Whether this is desirable or not is another matter. Maintaining an independence from fashion seems to me very valuable. I'd rather be a good poet with a day job than have had a good 'career' in poetry, whatever that means".

COLLECTIONS: *Parables and Faxes* (Bloodaxe, £6.95); *Cyfrif Un ac Un yn Dri* forthcoming from Barddas.

GOOD DOG!

All pets are part of one animal.
They look out at us from myriad eyes
hoping for food and a little love.
They themselves are unfailingly kind.
People who believe in reincarnation
feel the concern of departed relatives
shine from the heart of a new-born pup,
so confide in them, spoil them.
A well-placed "Om" in a mongrel's ear
can save the soul of a dying dog.

Ours is theologian. This one knows
that sticks in life are more reliable than cats
and that balls are better. Everything thrown
is instantly precious, well worth running for.
The river he loves and tends to wear
it often. A Baptist, he immerses himself
with total abandon so his otter soul
is renewed in the feeder with the bags of crisps
and ribbons of algae.
He wears the medal of himself with joy.

PETERLOO POETS

OPEN POETRY COMPETITION 1997

Sponsored by

MARKS & SPENCER

1st PRIZE £4,000
2nd PRIZE £1,000
3rd PRIZE £500   4th PRIZE £300
5th PRIZE £200   6th PRIZE £100

JUDGES:
Michael Donaghy • Helen Dunmore • Duncan Forbes • Harry Chambers

Michael Donaghy was born in New York. He was poetry editor for the *Chicago Review* before moving to London. His first collection, *Shibboleth* (OUP, 1988), won the Whitbread Poetry Prize, and the Geoffrey Faber Memorial Award of 1989.

Helen Dunmore has published six collections of poetry, of which the latest is *Recovering a Body* (Bloodaxe, 1994). Her third novel, *A Spell of Winter*, won the Orange prize for fiction.

Duncan Forbes has published four volumes of poetry: *August Autumn* (Secker & Warburg, 1984), *Public and Confidential* (Enitharmon, 1989), *Taking Liberties* (Enitharmon, 1993) and *Point the Finger* (The Bodley Head, 1994).

Harry Chambers, publisher of the Peterloo Poets imprint, reads all the poems submitted and supplies the other judges with a shortlist of 100 poems from which they select the prizewinners.

PREVIOUS WINNERS include Shafi Ahmed, Donald Atkinson, Debjani Chatterjee, David Craig, Anna Crowe, Carol Ann Duffy, Romesh Gunesekera, Mimi Khalvati, John Lyons, M.R. Peacocke, Rodney Pybus, Carol Shergold, David Simon, John Watts, Maureen Wilkinson, Chris Woods.

CLOSING DATE: Saturday 1st March 1997.   **RULES:** see overleaf.

RESULTS available Thursday 24th April 1997. All winning poems will be published in the *Peterloo Competition* poster/leaflet (June 1997) obtainable at £3.00 *post free*.

The poem winning the first prize of £4,000 will be published in *The Independent* on Thursday 24th April 1997.

✂---

ENTRY FORM

NAME: ....

ADDRESS: ....

....

Telephone no: ....   No. of Entries: ....(see overleaf)

Total entry fee enclosed of £ ....
Method of payment (delete as applicable): sterling cheque/P.O./Visa/Mastercard/Amex

Card No: .... Expiry date: .... Signature: ....

Entries to: **The Administrator, Peterloo Poetry Competition,
2 Kelly Gardens, Calstock, Cornwall PL18 9SA, U.K.**

Entrance fee: £4.00 sterling per poem: 10 poems maximum.
(Visa/Mastercard/Amex also accepted: supply card no. & expiry date plus your signature.) Foreign cheques/currency will not be accepted.

RULES OF ENTRY:

1. Entries must arrive on or before Saturday 1st March 1997. Results will be available on Thursday 24th April 1997.

2. No competitor may be under 16 years of age. No competitor may submit more than 10 entries. Entries must be accompanied by the appropriate fee (see above), payable to Peterloo Poets.

3. Poems may be on any subject or theme and in any style or form but must not have been previously published. All poems must be typewritten in the English language, be the unaided work of the competitor, and must not exceed 40 lines. **MANUSCRIPTS CANNOT BE RETURNED.**

4. The entry form overleaf should be completed with the competitor's name, address, telephone number and the number of poems entered. The titles of the poems must be listed on the reverse of the form. The competitor's name must **NOT** appear on the typescript.

5. Copyright remains with the author, but authors of prizewinning poems must agree to assign first publication rights to Peterloo Poets for inclusion in the *Peterloo Competition* poster/leaflet (June 1997, £3.00 post free: cheques payable to Peterloo Poets).

6. Receipt of entries will be acknowledged **ONLY** if entries are accompanied by a stamped, self-addressed postcard marked "Receipt". Individuals will be notified of the results **ONLY** if entries are accompanied by a stamped, self-addressed envelope marked "Results".

7. The organisers reserve the right to change the panel of judges without notice, and to withold payment of any or all prizes if the judges decide that such witholding is justified. The decision of the judges will be final and the organisers will not enter into any correspondence thereon.

8. Entries not complying with the rules of the competition will be disqualified, and the submission of any entry will be deemed to imply the unqualified acceptance of the rules of entry by the competitor.

✂---
TITLES OF POEMS SUBMITTED:

Subscribe now and receive this fifty-minute poetry cassette, worth £6.50, free.

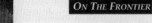

POETRY WALES

volume 31 number 2   £2.50

ON THE FRONTIER

Anne Stevenson:
Identity, Language and Welsh Poetry

Iwan Llwyd:
Springtime in Saskatoon

Gwyneth Lewis:
three new poems and an interview

Twentieth Century Anglo-Welsh Poetry

Edited by
Dannie Abse

DYLAN THOMAS	GILLIAN CLARKE
'Poem in October'	'Neighbours'
JOHN ORMOND	JOHN DAVIES
'Cathedral Builders'	'Sunny Prestatyn'
GLYN JONES	TONY CURTIS
'Again'	'Soup'
EDWARD THOMAS	TONY CONRAN
'Old Man'	'Elegy for the Welsh Dead
RUTH BIDGOOD	in the Falkland Islands, 1982'
'Hawthorn at Digiff'	ROBERT MINHINNICK
LESLIE NORRIS	'The Aerial'
'Elegy for David Beynon'	SHEENAGH PUGH
HARRI WEBB	'Do you think we'll ever get
'Synopsis of	to see earth, Sir?'
the Great Welsh Novel'	CATHERINE FISHER
IDRIS DAVIES	'Severn Bore'
'Gwalia Deserta XI'	JOHN TRIPP
ALUN LEWIS	'Connection in Bridgend'
'All Day It Has Rained ...'	GWYNETH LEWIS
JEAN EARLE	'Six Poems on Nothing: III'
'Jugged Hare'	DUNCAN BUSH
DANNIE ABSE	'Summer 1984'
'In the Theatre'	HILARY LLEWELLYN-WILLIAMS
	'Feeding the Bat'

Poetry Wales magazine was founded in 1965 to provide a platform for Welsh poets and poets living in Wales. All the writers on this cassette have featured in the magazine, as well as many others that could not be included here, from R.S. Thomas to Stephen Knight and Deryn Rees-Jones. We hope that you will enjoy this selection of poems by Anglo-Welsh poets, and that on turning to the pages of the magazine itself you will find an equally enjoyable mix of poets, with articles, interviews, new writing and new writers, translations, reviews and provocative editorials.

For more information about *Poetry Wales* or publications from Seren, please write to: Poetry Wales Press, First Floor, 2 Wyndham Street, Bridgend, CF31 1EF. The anthology *Twentieth Century Anglo-Welsh Poetry* is published by Seren in May 1997.

of Gwyneth Lewis,
Christine Evans,
Menna Elfyn, Jean Earle,
Maurice Riordan,
Katherine Pierpoint
and others

Twenty-two classic poems, chosen from the anthology *Twentieth Century Anglo-Welsh Poetry* and read by Dannie Abse and Siân James.

Cassette only available through *Poetry Wales*.
For information about the anthology, published May 1997, contact Seren at the address overleaf.

POETRY WALES

was founded in 1965 to provide a platform for poets living and writing in Wales. It continues to publish the best poets from Wales, including many featured on the cassette, together with poets from England, Ireland, Scotland, America, Australia and elsewhere, reviews, articles, translations, and provocative editorials.

"it may be that poetry, as the word used to be understood, is obsolete and will never again be wanted. The best poetry of the future may be dramatic, written for television. And why not?" – Anne Stevenson, PW 31.4

"exude[s] a scolding, finger-wagging preachiness that makes you want to rush out and harpoon something" – Sheenagh Pugh on *Whale Nation*, PW 31.2

"[Are] dead poets more interesting to critics than live ones? Their work is conveniently fixed of course. As are their corporeal remains: they're not going to come up to you and sock you on the jaw because they disliked what you said about them last month in the pages of X magazine. But if there are dangers in writing about living poets, there might also be unusual satisfactions." – Richard Poole, PW 31.3

"... everyone writes poetry, don't they? And if everyone writes poetry then poetry becomes almost sacrosanct. How dare you criticise poems I wrote about the death of my wife or my pet gibbon — they are how I really felt." – David Kennedy, PW 31.3

SUBSCRIPTIONS

Individuals: £10 a year; £18 for two years˙. Institutions: £15 a year

˙subscriptions for individuals will rise to £12 a year, £22 for two years, from April 1997
Contact Poetry Wales office address for overseas rates

I would like to subscribe to *Poetry Wales* for . . . year(s), and claim my free cassette.

I enclose a cheque/postal order for £. . . . . . .

Please debit my visa / access / mastercard.

Number ☐☐☐☐☐☐☐☐☐☐☐☐☐☐☐☐ Expiry Date . . . . . .

Name . . . . Address . . . . Postcode . . . . . .

send to *Poetry Wales* (Subscriptions), First floor, 2 Wyndham Street, Bridgend, CF31 1EF, Wales

His taste in art is for the Primitives.
He admires and collects all local sticks
and is a connoisseur of stones
which, being Staffordshire Bull, he eats.
He acquires the occasional traffic cone
for a hint of the abstract.
He finds that bushes all sprout balls,
mainly green and of the tennis kind,
a miraculous harvest which he daily reaps.

Something there is about a dog
draws conversation from frosty men

and available women. Trick for lonely boys
                                        and girls:
Get a dog. Walk him. For be it ugly or
                                    pure-bred,
a dog on a lead says: "Here is a love
that makes its bargain with bad habits and
                                        smells,
the brute in a person, can accommodate needs
far other than its own, allows for beastliness".

Some nights our lodger gets his favourite ball,
runs into the river and tramples the moon.

THE FLAGGY SHORE

(To Nora Nolan)

Not that this coastline's not a work of art
to those who watch it as the hay's
brought in to its stanzas before the rain,
barometer dropping, as the tide
laps at the easy-going carraigín
in the gardens of seaweed; as the heron stands
precisely on water then shrieks as it sees
its own reflection; as glossy cormorants
make metal eyes and dive like hooks
fastening the bodice of the folding tide;
as the ladies down for an evening walk
throw stones at the water and at their own lives
and the phone in an empty kiosk rings . . .
And it's not that we never wanted to know
that this is no place that we can stay
(or hope to remember in its indigo,
steel and vermilion) or be able to say
that it could protect us, or even recall
that we'd been there watching the currents' snakes
swim out to be drowned by an incoming squall.

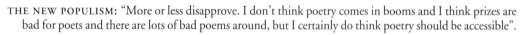

ALICE OSWALD

THE WAY INTO POETRY: "Age 8 – terrified at night and when morning came I was so pleased I wrote a crap little poem to celebrate and decided then to be a poet".

HEROINES AND HEROES: Ted Hughes, Gerard Manley Hopkins, Ian Hamilton Finlay, Dante, Homer, Hugh McDiarmid, David Jones.

CONTEMPORARY INFLUENCES: Ted Hughes, Iain Hamilton Finlay, John Ashbery ("slightly and only in a general way").

KEEPING UP? "No".

THE NEW POPULISM: "More or less disapprove. I don't think poetry comes in booms and I think prizes are bad for poets and there are lots of bad poems around, but I certainly do think poetry should be accessible".

NEW GENERATION POETS: "Negative".

WHY DO YOU THINK THERE ARE MORE GOOD WOMEN POETS PUBLISHING TODAY? "Contraception".

7 OUT OF 9 RECENT FORWARD FIRST COLLECTION WINNERS HAVE BEEN WOMEN: "No particular reason".

KEEPING THE DAY JOB? "Difficult – depends on the person. I still think it should be an under-cover job".

THE MELON GROWER

She concerned him,
but the connection had come loose.
They made shift with tiffs and silence.

He sowed a melon seed.
He whistled in the greenhouse.
She threw a slipper at him

and something jostled in the loam
as if himself had been layed blind.
She misperceived him. It rained.

The melon got eight leaves, it lolled.
She banged the plates.
He considered his fretful webby hands.

"If I can sex" he said "the flowers,
very gently I'll touch their parts
with a pollen brush made of rabbit hairs".

The carpels swelled. He had to prop them on pots.
She wanted the house repainting.
He was out the back watering.

He went to church, he sang "O Lord how long shall the wicked … ?"
He prayed, with his thumbs on his eyes.
His head, like a melon, pressured his fingers.

The shoots lengthened
and summer mornings came with giant shadows
and arcs as in the interim of a resurrection.

She stayed in bed, she was coughing.
He led the side-shoots along the wires.
She threw the entire tea-trolley downstairs.

And when the milk was off
and when his car had two flat tyres
and when his daughter left saying she'd had enough,

he was up a ladder hanging soft nets from the beam
to stop the fruit so labouring the stem.
The four globes grew big at ease

and a melony smell filled the whole place
and he caught her once, confused in the greenhouse,
looking for binder-twine. Or so she says.

LEAF

(for J.O. born 9.9.96)

the leaf that now lies being made
in its shell of scale; the hush of things
unseen inside; the flutter of dead wood;
the slow through-flow that feeds
a form curled under; hour by hour
the thick reissuing starlike shapes
of cells and pores and water-rods –
which builds up, which becomes a pressure,
a gradual fleshing out of a longing for light,
a small hand unfolding, feeling about . . .
into that hand the entire
object of the self being coldly placed,
the provisional, the inexplicable I
in mid-air, meeting the wind and dancing

'The Melon Grower' reprinted from Alice Oswald, *The Thing in the Gap-Stone Stile*
(Oxford Poets, 1996), by permission of Oxford University Press.

KATHERINE PIERPOINT

THE WAY IN: "Reading it as a search for experience and meaning-making (and as a child, loving the rhythm and rhyme)".

HEROINES AND HEROES: John Burnside, Pauline Stainer, Les Murray, Ivor Cutler, John Cooper Clarke, Seamus Heaney, Ted Hughes, Christopher Reid, Selima Hill, Michael Ondaatje.

KEEPING UP: Reads *Poetry Review*, review pages of weekly papers, occasionally *TLS, LRB, PN Review*.

NEW POPULISM: "Generally approve of promoting poetry more widely, especially projects which treat it honestly (i.e. accept that it may unsettle the reader, may not always be 'fun') eg. Poems on the Underground and Buses ... Concerned that 'populism' may focus mainly on performance poetry for instant impact, which is often more about drama – which is great, but only one segment of poetry".

THE WOMAN QUESTION: "There are more good women doing *everything* than ever before".

KEEPING THE DAY JOB? "It's not so much belief in hanging on to the day job as having to. A 'career' in poetry is possibly 80% gathering/dream/incubation time".

COLLECTION: *Truffle Beds* (Faber, £6.99).

FROG

The cat walks across the room on a line
Precisely strung between huge, shifting secrets

And drops a frog onto the carpet.
This is fierce, and it is utterly simple.
It cannot be changed.

The frog is soft as a coddled egg;
An egg with that shock of a fertile bloodspot,
That one red eye on its twisted string.
It is soft as a seahorse child extruded from the stomach,
Yellow and green. Liver-spotted as an old hand,
Semi-transparent in its ancient nakedness.

The frog calls out now,
It squats on the carpet; destitute, terrible,
In an agony of drought.
Its pale thread-fingers curl
Like newly-stripped flax, burning up in the cool air.
Branded by what is happening.

I'd thought that frogs were mainly silent
Or gave the odd, deep-bellied, cartoon croak
In the rum-punch evenings
Along the swamp, the steaming ponds.

This one cries. Pierced, and piercing.
Shrill with injustice
At desertion by its god.
Screams as it squats
While the heart punches almost out of its sides
Searching, hammering between the ribs,
Clumsy as a blunted needle.
The heart is all eyes and hands, swarming,
Trying to climb away,
Get over the sides of this place.
The glue has gone between inside and out,
Everything is slipping, or frozen, or scorched.

And again and again now, again, forever
The frog's thin screams tear through
From its stillness –

Screams in the lowered face of its tormentor
Up from the carpet, the static-sparking desert.

FENLAND STATION IN WINTER

The railway station in winter lies wide open on three sides;
A waiting mousetrap.
No creatures out in the hard fields,
The desert of blue-lipped ice.
The tracks tweeze the last thin train away,
Wipe it on the rim, and lose it.

The sky is bent so low now, the wind is horizontal.
It whittles the sky's undersurface to the pith,
Paring away a grey unwinding peel of snow.
A mean, needling flake rides the flat wind,
Picking the empty teeth of the trees,
Then falling, frantic, to gnaw at the setting earth,
Clinging there like a starving mouse's claws in velvet.

'Fenland Station in Winter' reprinted from Katherine Pierpoint, *Truffle Beds*,
by permision of Faber & Faber Ltd.

DERYN REES-JONES

THE WAY INTO POETRY: "Practically, through a weekly poetry workshop, set up by undergraduates at University College of North Wales, '87–'90".

HEROINES AND HEROES: Donne, Marvell, Denise Riley, Frank O'Hara, Elizabeth Bishop, Sylvia Plath.

INFLUENTIAL CONTEMPORARIES: Douglas Dunn, Eavan Boland, Gillian Clarke, Carol Ann Duffy, Medbh McGuckian, Jo Shapcott, Selima Hill.

KEEPING UP: Reads *London Magazine, Poetry Review, Poetry Wales, Verse*; reviews for *London Magazine, Poetry Review, Poetry Wales*; edited *Poetry Wales* 32/2.

NEW POPULISM: "I think National Poetry Day works as a good focus for poetry, but generally I think poetry shouldn't get confused with things I don't approve of, eg. competitiveness, marketing ploys, general razzmatazz. I don't think there is a new populism. I think the work done by poets in schools and communities is the most valuable thing".

NEW GENERATION POETS: "Interested in the work of the poets, instinctively wary of the 'marketing' side of things; and I did think the criteria were strange, leading to the exclusion of poets whose work has been very influential, eg. Sweeney and Shapcott".

7 OUT OF 9 RECENT FORWARD FIRST COLLECTION WINNERS HAVE BEEN WOMEN: "I have no idea why. It would be nice to think that it was simply because the judges thought they were the most interesting first collections".

KEEPING THE DAY JOB? "I don't think in terms of a career in poetry. Poetry is something that I do – I wish I could do it full-time. But I also feel lucky to have a full-time job which in some ways accommodates my other life. (I teach literature and creative writing)".

COLLECTIONS: *The Memory Tray* (Seren, £5.95). Essays: *Consorting with Angels: Modern Women Poets* (Bloodaxe, £10.95).

FROM HIS COY MISTRESS

"My early work is the fear of falling. Later on it became the art of falling. Falling without hurting yourself. Later on it is the art of hanging in there" – Louïse Bourgeois

Some days I think I will become a nun,
Book in a convent miles away,
Cut off my hair, and dress in black
Wanting to purge myself of men.

I'd kneel and pray and chant a lot,
Lie in a narrow bed, devising titles
Of unwritten books: *A Semiotics of Flirtation.*
Love? Some Concepts of the Verb "To Sin".

One thing's for sure, by wanting you
I'm not the woman that I think I am.
I cannot eat or sleep at all,
Just think about your lovely mouth,

The eerie moonlight and the Northern seas.
And hope my body's still the temple
That you'd come upon, as if by chance,
To excavate a hundred years from now,

Burn incense in and dance and sing,
Oh yes, and weeping, worship in.

WHAT IT'S LIKE TO BE ALIVE

(after Django Bates)

I remember the nights, and the sounds of the nights
and the moon, and the bossy clouds, then the clear sky
and the stars, the angels on the Rye

and I remember the way we knelt on the bed, how the bedclothes
were a tide, and the sunlight was a tide, and how everything pulled

and I remember the trains, leaving and arriving
and the nights

and I remember the tears, your tears, and my tears
and how we revere children, not lovers,
how the angels cried

and I remember your face and you coming
in my hands

and the clouds, and the stars, and how, for a moment,
with our eyes tight closed
how the planets lurched

and the angels smiled
and I remember how I did not know if this was grief or love

this hot pool in my hands
and the sounds
and then nothing.

A watermark held up to the light.
A boat rowed off the edge of the world.

RUTH SHARMAN

THE WAY INTO POETRY: "English teaching at school was such a dreary affair that I remained largely indifferent to the contents of Palgrave's *Golden Treasury*, fired instead by Biology lessons and Seneca's descriptions of Nero bleeding his mother to death over a hot bath. It was not until I went to university and began studying Baudelaire, Mallarmé and Rimbaud that I began to develop a real awareness of poetry, and even then I was slow to read works in English, making a tentative start with Thomas Hardy and John Clare. (There are still huge gaps waiting to be filled.) My first poetic jottings were prompted by my mother's sudden death when I was in my twenties and represented an attempt to come to terms with my feelings.

HEROINES AND HEROES: Robert Frost, Edward Thomas, Georg Trakl, Baudelaire, Philippe Jaccottet, Seamus Heaney, Michael Longley, Eavan Boland, Carol Ann Duffy and Vicki Feaver.

INFLUENTIAL CONTEMPORARIES: "The last three above, but in particular Vicki Feaver".

KEEPING UP: Reads *London Magazine, Poetry Review*, and others intermittently (eg. *The North, The Rialto, Staple*).

THE NEW POPULISM: "I approve, heartily – even if I found myself cringing at the glitzy *Top of the Pops* style presentation of the Nation's Ten Favourite Poems on TV. Poetry needs all the exposure it can get, and poets need money – so the more publicity and the more prizes the better. Once people have freed themselves of the notion that poetry is necessarily difficult, tedious or irrelevant to their daily lives, we'll have taken an important step away from the musty teaching methods that smother many a child's natural interest in poetry".

NEW GENERATION POETS: "Positive – for many of the same reasons as above. The Nation's Favourite Poems (however worthy) had a certain predictability about them and none (with the exception of Jenny Joseph's and Roger McGough's) was strictly contemporary. What is more, their poetic preoccupations seemed to reflect a largely middle-aged, or older, voting audience. We need to get young people interested in poetry and we need more promotions like the New Generation Poets to make the public aware of the many new voices speaking today in ways that are relevant to their lives and their concerns".

THE WOMAN QUESTION: "Women have always been sensitive to their surroundings and to the world of the emotions and have always had the potential to communicate their awareness. Recent generations of women have enjoyed the opportunity and the confidence to express their abilities in many different areas – including poetry. In turn there has been a response to and a recognition of the qualities which abound in women's poetry".

7 OUT OF 9 RECENT FORWARD FIRST COLLECTION WINNERS HAVE BEEN WOMEN: "Is it that editors, judges, and the public at large, are looking more and more to poetry to provide such qualities as concreteness of vision, sensuousness, emotional directness and are less impressed by the aggressive cleverness and hermeticism that has been the hallmark of so much modern (and often male) poetry?"

KEEPING THE DAY JOB? "A poetry career is not realistic – not unless you're Seamus Heaney or Fiona Pitt-Kethley, or are prepared to put in a great deal of hard graft as a creative writing tutor – which, I suspect, is inimical to the creative process itself. The right job, if it can only be found (in my case it's probably gardening), may even feed the poetic impulse".

COLLECTION: First collection forthcoming from Picador in Autumn 1997.

WOMAN DRYING HERSELF

(after Degas)

Her back is curved like a leaf
on one of those poplars
he wouldn't paint

moving freely in the wind,
catching light as it turns,
holding firmly to a stem

so strong and supple, you'd say
in other lives she might have bent
to lift potatoes from the soil

or forked in hay, whitened sheets,
ironed and folded, and walked
with children on her hips.

Where it dips to meet her spine
like hills down to a cleave
he gave her the colour

of sweetbriars and gorse stalks
charred by summer fires,
while light from an unseen source

has opalised her shoulderblade
and thigh, the curving
river of her arm.

One orange slipper, a hint of
auburn hair, and a hundred years on
she breathes and burns

while the man who made her
shunned the sunlight
because it hurt his bloodshot eyes.

ARACHNOPHOBIA

There seems to be no cure
– not even in knowing
that a Frenchman spun
socks from the silk

or that in Colombia
they're said to piggyback
the souls of the dead
up to heaven:

there can be no truce
with wolf or widow
(her belly bulging
like a Gladstone bag)

or the one that weaves
a subterranean lair
and lines it with silk
and listens at the door

or even the harvestman
I saw sucking red juices
out of a beetle's back
in a field of alpine flowers.

I imagine bathfuls,
dream them falling
from rafters
in a run-down house

feel their squiggling legs
in the bed, swarming
under night clothes, probing
into eyes, ears, nose

furring the inside
of my mouth and running down
my throat, so when I call
to my mother

the sound dies
amidst the blackness
of a million million
minute hairs.

My Leaky Coracle

CAROL RUMENS EXTOLS THE VIRTUES OF WOMEN
"BEING BLOODY MISERABLE AND NOT IN CONTROL"

Making for Planet Alice

Edited by Maura Dooley
Bloodaxe, £8.95
ISBN 1 85224 398 8

IN HER INTRODUCTION, Maura Dooley says she wants to see women's poetry become "part of the main canon of English Literature". I had a comparable ambition when I edited *Making for the Open* twelve years ago. Now I see how futile it was. Such work is perceived inevitably as a criticism of, and alternative to, the canon. Dooley should realise she has chosen a self-defeating route to her goal, one practically guaranteed never to arrive.

A woman's anthology is *ipso facto* concerned with politics, weasel-words like celebration notwithstanding. And, of course, with economics. So let's say it loud and clear: anthologies of poetry by women sell. The publisher gets rich (though the poets and editors do not) and simultaneously earns good conduct stars. Meanwhile, the reputation of Women Poets (the glamorous, saleable product) and the stuff they actually write blurs into an unfathomable if vaguely fashionable mass which may actually prevent individual poets – and more importantly, poems – from emerging.

Again, Dooley is self-contradictory. She claims not to have wanted "to contemplate an anthology that might exclude the male reader, creating a separate culture for the writers included". As anyone not living on Planet Alice must realise, a woman's anthology has a *keep out* notice on it as far as the average male reader is concerned. Men rarely read such books, and never edit them. Women's anthologies are read primarily by women. They could even be viewed as the up-market version of the woman's magazine. The high graphic input in the Bloodaxe product – the mug-shot of each poet, the eye-catching cover-girl – reinforces the similarity. The women's anthology feeds some of the same desires – our curiosity about other women; our insecure need to see our own experiences reflected and to hear voices and sense attitudes we are at home with; our simultaneous wish for mould-breaking heroines.

I am not entirely deploring this. It may not rule out good poetry; the sense of a hungry readership can be artistically empowering. However, the readership needs to be sophisticated enough to demand linguistic adventure and ingenuity. Only then will the intertextual dialogue add savour to the verse – as it currently does in the literary community centred in, and radiating from, Northern Ireland, for example.

There are unquestionably some very good poets in this collection, though there are some rather amateurish ones. Among the dozen or so who should be commanding an attention independent of the W-word are Elizabeth Garrett, Lavinia Greenlaw, Maggie Hannan, Siobhan Morrissey, Ruth Padel, Katherine Pierpoint, Susan Wicks. Some of the poets are relatively well known, as this list illustrates: and some appeared, even with the same poems, in the predecessor anthology, *New Women Poets*, edited by myself in the late '80s. Are they pleased to have been twice-dubbed the new poets of their time? Isn't there something faintly deplorable in the idea that poets belong only to the decade or two of their first emergence? Many of us are still getting to grips with the modernity of a poet who died in 1886: her name was Emily Dickinson.

The question of whether there is a "womanly" aesthetic, however deliberately constructed, remains unanswered. Some of the ablest writers here are formalist, proudly refuting that old nonsense about women being barred, or obliged to bar themselves, from the symmetrical or linear. Elizabeth Garrett, in 'The Womanhood', writes verse steeped in traditional rhetoric. At the same time she appears to be almost directly describing that banal (and extremely male-orientated) version of femininity symbolised by the pert, sensual, wounded little face staring through the cracked Plexiglas on the cover of this book. She is a very skilled poet, but I wonder about her easy attribution of power to such a symbol: "Subtleties she practised / Till they had her by heart – / Played her like the psaltery / so no man could part / Her fingers' lattice / From their naked art. / It was the flame's syllable / And the ferryman's fee. / She sang men to heaven / Where she turned them free / With the taste of the obol / Where her name should be". The woman on the cover represents Marilyn Monroe, whose pitiable fate was indeed "the taste of the obol where her name should be".

Other writers do seem to favour looser constructions, metaphorical clusters, and an altogether more synaesthetic (therefore less "linear") approach. The vague shapes of what might be a womanly aesthetic in the making are discernible in work by Sarah Maguire, Ruth Padel, Tracey Herd. But it might be truer to say that the best writers are most like themselves. Is Maggie Hannan's linguistic virtuosity "male", "female" or simply "Hannan"?

Interestingly, light verse-with-an-edge might be emerging as the quintessentially female genre. Sophie Hannah and Eleanor Brown are writing in the tradition re-established in the 1980s by Wendy Cope (though not yet with Cope's finesse) which can be traced back to Dorothy Parker and earlier, English, "bluestocking" wits. Writers not working exclusively in this genre, but sometimes approaching it, include Gwyneth Lewis and Kate Clanchy. That the most traditional means – full rhyme, regular metre – are so often employed to tease and interrogate the most contemporary issues of sexual politics is a mystery. Is it because the addressee is usually male that the claws are so daintily gloved?

Radical feminists should prick up their ears when Jane Holland asserts "I am not a woman poet. / I am a woman and a poet. / The difference is in the eyes" – even if the issue is not as new, or as daylight clear, as this suggests. Each to her enabling myth. There's no good reason why women should write about (in Holland's negative iconography) "motherhood", "cunt" or "breast", except that such topics genuinely enthral them. At the same time, a poem is the product of an organism: it is no more independent of biochemistry than it is of history and politics. Most male writers (not all!) have till now written as if such detachment were possible,

Sappho through English Poetry, edited by Peter Jay and Caroline Lewis, was recently published by Anvil.

but this has not prevented the creation of works of great literary value.

Women writers are currently drawing sustenance from canonical sources. Their literary role-models are not necessarily women. Their subjects are as likely to be air-travel and mathematics as childbirth. But there is no taboo on the personal or domestic: neither should there be. Probably the achievement has very little to do with "women being positive, creative, and in control of their own lives", as the introduction has it. Poems cannot emerge from total enslavement, of course, but they do not come out of girl-guide accomplishment, either. What about being bloody miserable and not in control: isn't that what the muse often seems to favour? Yet the insistence on transgression is just as bad. The title of this anthology makes me uneasy: it suggests that the infantile and the imaginative are interchangeable, rather than that they merely have points in common. It highlights a soft-surreal, romantic-nostalgic poem by Deryn Rees-Jones which pleads: "Quietly, quietly / Take me to that strange place, by bus, by unicycle, / Helicopter, aeroplane. Let me sail to Planet Alice in my heart, / My leaky coracle, let me circumnavigate the moon, / The foam of snow white stars" (etc.). Neither the rhythm nor the imagery here has the verve ostensibly being celebrated. There was a time, I believe, for splitting the world of the canon open, for bringing in the new voices, the raw and awkward and anarchic. But there is a time, too, for consolidation, stringency, sifting. This book would be better if it were leaner. Bloodaxe, of course, would not agree. First, we had *Sixty Women Poets* (admittedly representing three generations): now, we have thirty poets representing the first half of the '90s. What will it be next – 2000 Women Poets for the Year 2000? Such profligacy does not benefit women writers: it may in fact ensure that, as far as posterity is concerned, the great and the good will once more, thanks to their gender, be "hidden from history".

Sylvia Plath's Word Games

ANNE STEVENSON'S LAST WORD ON A POET
WHO RELISHED LANGUAGE AS A SOURCE OF ENJOYMENT

EVERYBODY KNOWS HER story, and a great many readers have been excited and disturbed by her writings. How much have the dramatic details of Sylvia Plath's life contributed to the climate of awed veneration that has been generated by her poetry? What would we think of her today had she lived into her sixties, the famous author, doubtless, of eight or ten volumes of verse and a shelf of fiction?

Such questions, unanswerable as they are, come naturally to mind when we consider Sylvia Plath's published work – I mean all of it: letters, journals, prose and poetry – from a distance of over thirty years; more years than the poet lived. Given her countless admirers and their continued interest in everything pertaining to her, it may be useful to separate out the reality of Plath's achievement from some of the hearsay that obscures it. As I see it, there are three main roots (routes) that invite exploration.

First of all, yes, we must take into consideration the circumstances of the poet's life and self-inflicted death. Although it would be simplistic to pigeon-hole Plath as a "confessional" poet, there is no doubt she wrote, at least on one level, straight out of experience. She had, so her mother tells us, an extraordinary memory. She never forgot. One could say that in a Borgesian way she was cruelly compelled to remember everything that happened to her. All her writings therefore teem with private images: her Winthrop childhood, Cape Cod summers, strawberry- and spinach-picking; movies she saw of the war; traumatic incidents, such as being admitted to a cadaver room and looking at embryos in jars of formaldehyde, together with lesser ones like observing a dead pig, watching an owl, picking a rose, sewing red material into curtains. A few ineradicable experiences – losing her father, going mad, undergoing electro-convulsive therapy, haemorrhaging when she lost her virginity, giving birth – surge again and again into her work. Unless a reader knows something of this poet's biography many of her references will be lost.

Her private experiences, of course, would be of no importance if she had not, in poem after poem – and this is my second point – imaginatively trans-formed, exaggerated and brilliantly dramatised them. Ted Hughes's interest in Christian and pre-Christian myth, augmented by her own fascinated readings of Graves, Lawrence, Jung and Freud, profoundly affected Plath's impressionable mind. She seems really to have believed that her individual life was sacrificially in thrall to ineluctable archetypal forces. Her journal of January 3, 1959, for example, refers to the "great, stark bloody play acting itself out over and over again behind the sunny facade of our daily rituals" (*Bitter Fame*, p. 148). It was some such fatalistic myth, some idea of powers beyond her control that were governing her life, that, in my view, dictated her last poems.

Once it is understood that a palingenetic scheme of death and rebirth is central to all Plath's major work, it is simple enough to identify within it a consistent system of symbols: doubles in mirrors or pools, drownings, burnings, burials, a dead ghostly father and his bees, an ever-present, bitterly resented mother, nullifying statues, shape-changing witches, and puppet master of them all, the ambiguous figure of the moon – the bald nurse cum disquieting muse of her private mythology. Many of these recurring signatures are linked, moreover, to colours, such as red (life), white (deathly stasis), black (annihilation), green (spring, but also poison) and so forth. Those who are fascinated by the myth will find in Judith Kroll's *Chapters in a Mythology* (1976) a reliable guide to its iconography. Kroll stresses, too, the poet's immense debt to the visual arts. One way to teach Plath's poems would be to ask students to make paintings of them.

Finally, though, we must acknowledge that Sylvia Plath, from her earliest years, put her writing on a par with her life, and when we turn to that writing, one of the first things we notice is how much this self-making maker of myths was indebted to other writers with whom she put herself to school. All her life she was a deeply serious, fanatically obsessed student. Sometimes consciously, sometimes unconsciously, she "hooked" images and ideas from books she intimately knew (many of them children's books) or from literature she had scrupulously studied, underlined and memorised. How deeply she was indebted to T. S. Eliot I hope partially to demonstrate. But she was equally indebted to the work of D. H. Lawrence, Dylan Thomas, Yeats, Auden, Theodore Roethke, while technically she imitated James Joyce, whose tricks with words she could perform as well as he could.

Perhaps it is a measure of Plath's originality that the loot she indefatigably pinched from her literary forebears has never been much noticed. One of her objects, I'm pretty sure, was to contain or reformulate the classics of the past in a bid, like Eliot's, to refresh and remould the tradition. Nothing if not a modernist, Sylvia Plath, in my view, deserves fame for her literary skill, for technical cleverness, musicality, economy of diction and a keen wit – achievements that would eventually have made her name as a mature writer had not psychological illness and a too personally interpreted myth driven her to kill herself. Rather than concentrate further on the personal tragedy of this remarkable poet, I hope scholars will find time in the future to study her language and the way in which her writings tie into and reinforce major themes in *her* work and *our* time. For there is no denying that twentieth-century high culture, which began so hopefully in an era of innovative triumph, now seems itself on the point of committing suicide out of what looks like pique, or an attack of *fin-de-siècle* exhaustion.

I was first alerted to the amount of T. S. Eliot Plath incorporated into her writing by a not-very-complimentary review. *Bitter Fame*, wrote the reviewer, culpably failed to connect an abandoned title for Plath's first book of poems with Eliot's 'Ash Wednesday'. True enough, 'The Devil of the Stairs' comes from part III of Eliot's poem: "At the first turning of the second stair / I turned and saw below / The same shape twisted on the banister / Under the vapour in the fetid air / Struggling with the devil of the stairs ..."

At around the same time (1958–9) Plath also considered borrowing a phrase from Eliot's *Four Quartets* and using it as the title of a short story. The story was finally called 'The Daughters of Blossom Street'. 'The Earth Our Hospital', however, initially struck the author as appropriate – taken from Eliot's lyric for Good Friday ('East Coker' part IV): "The whole earth is our hospital / Endowed by the ruined millionaire". Since "millionaire" crops up in 'Stopped Dead' as well as (rather exaggeratedly) in a good many of Plath's letters and journals, it is possible that Eliot helped to furnish her mind with the word – along with other Plathic familiars: the surgeon, the nurse, Adam, mental wires (nerves), fever, roses, flames and the eucharistic blood and flesh of Eliot's hymn. Very likely Sylvia Plath knew part IV of 'East Coker' by heart.

In it, Eliot's "wounded surgeon", a figure of Christ, operates on the body of Christianity lying "distempered" under his "bleeding hands". The second stanza introduces "a dying nurse" whose care it is to keep Christianity's disease instrumental to its health, reminding us of "Adam's curse" and insisting that "to be restored, our sickness must grow worse". It is at this point that the famous lines about "the earth our hospital" occur, "endowed by the ruined millionaire" – that is, by a God bankrupt in the world he created, who ordains that "if we do well" we will die (and thus be saved) of the "absolute paternal care" that has given us life. Finally, two paradoxical stanzas reassert the palingenetic myth at the heart of the Christian mystery. It is striking how Plath-like Eliot's succession of images is:

The chill ascends from feet to knees,
The *fever* sings in *mental wires*.
If to be warmed, then I must freeze
And quake in frigid purgatorial *fires*
Of which the *flame is roses*, and the *smoke is briars*.

Plathian words are italicised. For Plath's burning roses, see also George Macdonald's children's tale, *The Princess and the Goblin*. For briars, read hooks. Eliot continues

The *dripping blood* our only drink,
The *bloody flesh* our only food . . .

Of course we can't single out Eliot's hymn, in its unmistakable Christian context, as the only source of Plath's imagery. Roses and – or as – flames, usually with sexual implications, run all though the Western poetic tradition, as Plath well knew. Yet, though not specifically Christian, the terms of Plath's death-and-resurrection myth hardly eschewed Christian iconography. Remember how often she had recourse to the "Communion tablet" – even while rejecting it. If you trace the Communion wafer through her work, you soon see that it stands for a whole class of words having to do with eating (accepting) as likewise and significantly for its opposite, revulsion (rejecting). In 'Medusa', for example:

Who do you think you are?
A Communion wafer? Blubbery Mary?

Later, she cried out in 'Totem', "Let us eat it like Plato's afterbirth, / Let us eat it like Christ . . ." (Christ, here, must be Plato's afterbirth); and, in 'Mystic', "What is the remedy? / The pill of the Communion tablet . . . ?"

"Adam's curse" would have been familiar to Plath from Yeats as well as Eliot – as in "Side of green Adam" in 'Purdah'. See also "mud . . . / Thick, red and slipping. It is Adam's side" in 'Getting There'. Ted Hughes says Plath knew that the name Adam means "red earth", so it's pretty certain she consciously made a connection between the biblical reference and the blood-coloured Devon soil from which Eve/Plath in 'Getting There' is being (re)born. Indeed, there was no reason why this poet should not make use of every bit of mytho-poetical language she could lay her hands on. Eliot believed that to bring other poets back to life was one of the perennial tasks of modern criticism. Even a compar-

atively early poem such as 'The Stones' can be considered, in one of its aspects, as a comment on and criticism of Eliot that brings a she-Christ back to life in a questioning, perhaps even sceptical frame of reference.

Love is the uniform of my *bald nurse*,
[skull of the risen god/goddess]
Love is the bone and sinew of my *curse*.
[Adam's/Eve's fall]
The vase, reconstructed, houses
The *elusive rose* . . .
[redemption through love]

(My italics)

Plath, of course, was recounting her own emergence from spiritual death and purgatorial suffering. It would have been natural for her to feminise and adapt the older poet's rituals for the ceremony of her rebirth. In her last poem, 'Edge' the rose recurs, together with the bald nurse-moon, but here the flower is killed by the skull-like moon's crackling blacks (its eye-and-mouth sockets) that, despite poetry and its healing "blood jet", are dragging the poet for ever out of the rose garden:

She has folded

Them [her children] back into her body as petals
Of a rose close when the garden

Stiffens and odors bleed
From the sweet, deep throats of the night flower.

The moon has nothing to be sad about,
Staring from her hood of bone.

She is used to this sort of thing.
Her blacks crackle and drag.

'The Bee Meeting', too, makes undercover reference to Eliot. Here is the "sacred grove" transformed into a garden rank with hawthorn that "etherizes" its children (as in that famous line from 'Prufrock') followed by a passage describing ordinary neighbours and bee-keepers as ritually attired priests or celebrants. Simultaneously, they are robed patients gathered in expectation of a surgeon who will perform a vital yet almost certainly fatal operation:

They are leading me to the shorn grove, the circle of
hives
Is it the hawthorn that smells so sick?

The barren body of hawthorn, etherizing its children.
Is it some operation that is taking place?
It is the surgeon my neighbors are waiting for.
This apparition in a green helmet,
Shining gloves and white suit . . .

Ted Hughes testifies that Plath everywhere combined Eliot's sacrificial myths with those of D. H. Lawrence, whose fable 'The Man Who Died' had made a powerful impression upon her when she was at Cambridge. "I was the woman who died", she wrote in August 1953, referring to Lawrence's resurrected, sexual Christ cum Osiris, "and I came in touch through Sassoon [a former lover] with that flaming of life, that resolute fury of existence . . ."

In the pre-*Ariel* poems, Eliot's rhythm and diction tended to overlay Lawrence's thematic matter. (Though it could be argued, too, that Plath's more plaintive *Ariel* voice to some extent echoes Lawrence's in his last poems.) Not only did Plath in 'The Bee Meeting' snip bits from Eliot's vocabulary; she adopted, in the interrogative mood, the very syntax and sounds of 'Prufrock', mixing it with echoes from the vegetation ceremony in 'East Coker'. Listen to the short i combined with s and t that spikes the rhetorical questions in 'The Bee Meeting': *is it, is it?* straight out of 'Prufrock': "Oh, do not ask, 'what is it?' / Let us go and make our visit". Further examples of hissing noises are rife in Plath's mockery (perhaps) of Eliot's portentousness in her poem 'A Birthday Present'.

What *is this*, behind this veil, *is it* ugly, *is it* beautiful?
It is shimmering, *has it* breasts, *has it* edges?

. . . *"Is this* the one I am to appear for,
Is this the elect one, the one with black eye-pits and a
scar?"
(My italics)

'A Birthday Present', indeed, seems an absolute present to the feminists amongst us, who will correctly read it as an attack on the entire patriarchal tradition. Lies, lies, lies, the poem cries, like the rest of history. How cleverly, though, Plath plays with her pastiche of Eliot's tone. I take "it" in this poem to stand for some terrible sacrificial truth hidden in the veils of social orthodoxy (present giving). The conclusion recasts Eliot's Christian myth in Plath's characteristically iconoclastic mould. Veils and shroudings are among her recurrent images, habitual distress-signals belonging to the Plathian code.

Only let down the veil, the veil, the veil.
If it were death
I would admire the deep gravity of it, its timeless eyes.
I would know you were serious . . .

The way in which Plath used signs and sounds to suggest connections she liked to make with literary tradition – even when she attacked it – was brought to my attention by an English scholar, Mrs. C. G. Richmond. To be fair, Mrs. Richmond, not I, should be presenting a paper on Sylvia Plath's word games, for Mrs. Richmond – who first studied Plath as a mature student about twenty years ago – believes that all Plath's poems were constructed according to a system encoded in their texts, a cryptic game based on Roget's *Thesaurus* that, given persistence and a gift for detection, can be discovered by any devotee patient enough to follow a trail of deliberately laid clues. I'm not sure I go along with all Mrs. Richmond's ideas, but they are certainly interesting. She suggests, for instance, that Plath often used sounds to suggest names for fictional characters. Disguises for Eliot would include "Elly Higgenbottom" and "Elaine" in *The Bell Jar*, "Ella Mason and her Eleven Cats", "Ellen" in 'The Baby Sitters', "Ellen" in the short story 'Day of Success' and "Nellie Meehan" in the story 'All the Dead Dears'. Recurrent in Plath's writing are sounds such as el, eli, li, lee; ie. em*bell*ish, bell, smell, *del*icate, sleep – all cryptograms for Eliot.

Well, perhaps. Plath did admire James Joyce, and many of her early poems are indeed cleverly executed Joycian exercises. Later poems, however, give evidence that her borrowings were more straightforward. The opening of 'Poem for a Birthday', written at Yaddo in 1959, echoes, for example, one of Eliot's 'Choruses from The Rock'. Here is Plath's 'Who?':

The month of flowering's finished. The fruit's in,
Eaten or rotten. I am all mouth.
October's the month for storage.

And here is Eliot's second 'Chorus':

Of all that was done in the past, you eat the fruit,
either rotten or ripe.
And the Church must be forever building, and always
decaying, and always being restored.

It's hard not to conclude that Plath has taken Eliot's Christian symbol literally and used "fruit" as a building block in her own mythology. "All mouth" in the same sequence we know was borrowed from Jung, while the structural "feel" of the poem shadows Theodore Roethke's 'The Lost Son', which Plath read seemingly for the first time at Yaddo that autumn.

Whatever her debt to Eliot and Roethke, 'Poem for a Birthday' surely represents Plath's first serious attempt to transmute her experience of madness and the "death" and "rebirth" that followed her 1953 suicide attempt into art. And clearly, as a work of art, the seven-part sequence exemplifies the modernist practice of piecing together a text out of copious borrowings from the culture's word-hoard. Plath also, of course, added to the mix some goodly chunks of her own. Defoe's dragon-like disease-carrying monsters of infected breath from *A Journal of the Plague Year* become inhabitants of the vast lake of dreams Plath invokes in 'Johnny Panic and the Bible of Dreams' – and that dream lake, as Ted Hughes confirms, was an actual nightmare Plath experienced in terrifying detail.

Sometimes Sylvia Plath's almost perfect memory got in her way. In her Journal of 1959, for example, she complained of remembering too much. "Lines occur to me and stop dead: 'The tiger lily's spotted throat'. And then it is an echo of Eliot's 'The tiger in the tiger pit' to the syllable and the consonance". True enough, Eliot's 'Lines for an Old Man' begins "The tiger in the tiger pit / Is not more irritable than I, / The whipping tail is not more still, / Than when I smell the enemy / Writhing in the essential blood / or dangling from the friendly tree …" Light verse? Nevertheless, Eliot's black joke puts in a prior claim, not only for Plath's tiger, but for the gigantic class of words she associated with blood; as also for her (partly) Tarot-inspired hanging man, and her madness. Like all modern poets, she confronted the aggravating, sometimes insuperable problem of writing in a tradition in which almost every word is a hand-me-down.

The tiger has a long history in literature. Lewis Carroll's tiger lily in *Alice Through the Looking Glass* would seem to be one of Plath's unconscious sources; and there was Blake's 'Tyger' of course, not to mention Shakespeare's Henry V advising his soldiers to imitate the tiger at Agincourt. Plath, like Eliot before her, would have been familiar with Kipling's fables and verses. Yet, despite many precedents, Plath did not hesitate to work the tiger lily,

at least, into that unforgettable and very beautiful poem to her baby son, 'The Night Dances'.

Paying close attention to Plath's literary sources and verbal facility directs attention away from her personal drama and focuses it on her very considerable wit. A vein of wit runs through all her work, though in the *Ariel* poems (note that her title again relates to a group of Eliot's poems) it tends to convert to cynicism, or sometimes, as in 'Medusa', to cruel raucous attack. When she first read 'Daddy' and 'Lady Lazarus' to A. Alvarez she described them – to his amazement – as "light verse". Much of her early work – poems she wrote while she was at Cambridge, for instance – can be understood as tough-worded humour. Look, for example, at 'Natural History' – number fifty-six in the *Collected Poems*.

> That lofty monarch, Monarch Mind,
> Blue-blooded in coarse country reigned;
> Though he bedded in ermine, gorged on roast,
> Pure Philosophy his love engrossed:
> While subjects hungered, empty-pursed,
> With stars, with angels, he conversed
> Till, sick of their ruler's godling airs,
> In one body those earthborn commoners
> Rose up and put royal nerves to the rack:
> King Egg-Head saw his domain crack,
> His crown usurped by the low brow
> Of the base, barbarous Prince Ow.

The whole poem is a joke based on the old saw about the philosopher who couldn't reason away his toothache. (There never was philosopher who could patiently abide the toothache.) Its anti-intellectualism is perhaps a trifle crude, owing something, maybe, to Yeats, something to the Elizabethans she was studying at Cambridge at the time, a good deal, perhaps, to Ted Hughes and Lucas Myers, with whom she regularly exchanged poems.

C. G. Richmond believes that Plath's texts all hide a "serious discussion of something else" which ought to be looked for when they seem superficially obscure. Puns and portmanteau-words, she thinks, conceal references to what is often called "something else" outright: "Hard gods were there, nothing else. / Still he thumbed out *something else*" ('The Hermit at Outermost House'); "*Something else* / Hauls me through air …/ Dead hands, dead stringencies" ('Ariel'); "All day, gluing my church of burnt matchsticks, / I dream of *someone else* entirely" ('The Jailor'); "This is not death, it is *something safer*" ('Flute Notes from a Reedy Pond').

Now, it may be, as Mrs. Richmond suggests, that this "something else" is nothing less than the entire body (or canon) of western literature to which Plath knew her work would some day belong. On the other hand, a more likely source of this reiterated "something else" was Plath's continual complaint in her journals of dissatisfaction with what she was writing. "These poems do not live: it's a sad diagnosis", she wrote in the poem 'Stillborn'. Ted Hughes is right, I think, when he suggests that before she secured in 'Elm' the *Ariel* voice that began to emerge in 'Poem for a Birthday' she was infuriatingly gnawed by a feeling that she ought to be writing about *something else*.

So without entirely agreeing with Mrs. Richmond, we can be grateful for her close readings, particularly of early poems, that show us how important "something else" always was to Sylvia Plath. When she was in college she could well have associated "something else" with poetry she judged to be more successful than her own. We know she carried the poems of Dylan Thomas around with her "like sacred talismans". And here again, the relationship between Plath's often contorted syntax and that of Dylan Thomas – an even more potent influence on her early work than Eliot – could do with some careful looking into. Equally, when we read in Plath "I Am Vertical / But I would rather be horizontal", it's as well to remember how familiar she was with the poems of W. H. Auden, who dedicated his *Poems 1927–1931* to Christopher Isherwood with this wry quatrain:

Let us honour if we can
The vertical man.
Though we value none
But the horizontal one.

I am suggesting, in other words, that Plath took her ideas of what poetry should be from the influential modernists she admired: Joyce, on whom she would have written her college thesis had she not broken down in 1953, as well as T. S. Eliot, D. H. Lawrence, Dylan Thomas, W. H. Auden and even Ezra Pound whose 'Ballad of the Goodly Fere', meaning mate or brother in middle English, says Mrs. Richmond, just may have induced her to play with its phonic twin, "fear", in the chorus of 'Johnny Panic'.

The only thing to love is Fear itself.
Love of Fear is the beginning of wisdom.
The only thing to love is Fear itself
May Fear and Fear and Fear be everywhere...

Love of "fear" would then, subliminally, imply brotherly love, and if so, the rhyming chant might appear to be more palatable than we had supposed. I myself believe such a reading to be wide of the mark. Fear, the "panic bird" of the stories and poems that preceded the bold confrontations of *Ariel*, was too much this poet's presiding genius to admit of much word-play. But Mrs. Richmond's approach should not be ignored, either. She shows us again and again how for Plath language was a relished source of enjoyment as well as a means of charting the tragedy of an attempted salvation.

In these late days of the century, our ideas of what Plath intended to do in poetry have in many instances been distorted by postmodernist language-theory and/or political emotion. A general desire to establish an independent women's tradition, for example, has persuaded some women critics to make pronouncements about Plath's psyche, personal habits and sexual orientation on wholly imaginary evidence. If Sylvia Plath was a major poet, she was not just a major woman poet, nor would she have wanted, I believe, to be enthroned in a women's ghetto.

True, in her last year she indeed turned the cannon of her scholarship and prosodic skill against the "male tradition" she had up until then energetically emulated. To do this, she made use of every bit of traditional lore she could lay hands on, visibly rejoicing in wordplay and sly literary references. What any and every aspiring woman poet ought to learn from Sylvia Plath, it seems to me, is how to overhear, imitate, play variations on and eventually transmute the English tradition in a wholly original and effective way. Sylvia Plath wasn't *democratic* about her feminism any more than Emily Dickinson or Elizabeth Bishop – or even Marianne Moore who went out of her way, at one time, to slap the ambitious young Plath down. I should like to suggest that closely studying Plath's language, vocabulary and literary borrowings, as Mrs. Richmond has, unnoticed and unacknowledged over the years, is a rewarding and enriching approach to her work. In a recorded interview at Yale (18 April 1958) Sylvia Plath described the way she herself set about writing poetry:

Technically I like to be extremely musical and lyrical, with a singing sound. I don't like poetry that just throws itself away in prose. I think there should be a kind of constriction and a kind of music, too. And again, I like the idea of managing to get wit in with the idea of seriousness, and contrasts, ironies, and I like visual images, and I like just good mouthfuls of sound which have meaning ... I lean very strongly toward forms that are I suppose, quite rigid in comparison certainly to free verse. I'm much happier when I know that all my sounds are echoing in different ways throughout the poem.

Well, there you have it. Together with her literary inheritance, those "good mouthfuls of sound", that wit with seriousness and the musical constrictions and forms of Plath's poetry will take us all, I believe, a long way along the road to understanding – and enjoying it.

With acknowledgements to Ted Hughes and C. G. Richmond for helpful advice.

Anne Stevenson's new *Collected Poems* is reviewed on p. 58 by Helen Dunmore.

ANNE STEVENSON
WHY TAKE AGAINST MYTHOLOGY? (1)

That twilight skyline, for example,
the more I look at it,
the more I see a skull
crushed into the hill, nose
chipped flat, jaw
thrust up, full bush
of genitals stirring just
in the right place.

See him? No, stand here,
clear of the house.
Now, uncork some
magnum of imagination!
Inflame your heart
with my enchanted giant.
Figure his resurrection
in your dreams, or art.

But make him art, not fact.
For when daylight comes back
it will cleave him apart.
And how could you love or believe
in a Wales made of ice-
cut rock? No sleep
in the reason for mountains,
no mind in the dark?

WHY TAKE AGAINST MYTHOLOGY? (2)

Why in the dark of your mind
do you persist
in personifying natural events?
That's not imagination, it's
arrogance – locating fate in stars,
off-loading guilt on rocks
that were liquid once, eons
before our blind unpurposeful cells

commenced their amphibious crawl.
You like to imagine? Imagine nuclei
moiling themselves alive in steamy
crevices, continents travelling
and clashing, a grinding
plain of ice, a Pleistocene caul,
gouging, sculpting, furrowing
this scoop of valley.

Before art, lichens delicately
etched that cliff face. Millions of
millennia made bracken, heather, gorse.
Such facts really do have to be
imagined! More than self-love
or a brief human crisis. Think of *us*
if truly you fancy giants asleep in moss
or minds in darkness!

JO SHAPCOTT
THETIS

Thetis was a sea godess who had the marvellous ability to change her shape.
Peleus, a young man who had failed to win her over by persuasion, was
taught by Proteus the way to overcome her: to bind her and hold on tightly
whatever shape she took. The result of the union was Achilles.

No man can frighten me: watch as I stretch
my limbs for the transformation, I'm laughing
to feel the surge of other shapes beneath my skin.
It's like this: here comes the full thrill of my art
as the picture of a variegated
lizard insinuates itself into my mind.
I extend my neck, lengthen fingers, push
down toes to find the form. My back begins
to undulate, the skin to gleam. I think
my soul has slithered with me into this
shape as real as the little, long tongue in my mouth,
as the sun on my back, as the skill in absolute stillness.
My name is Thetis Creatrix and you,
voyeur, if you looked a little closer, would see
the next ripples spread up my bloody tail, to bloom
through this changing spine as the bark begins
to harden over my trunk. Already
I am so much the oak I lean everything towards
the black oxygen in the black air, I process
delicious gases through my personal chemistry,
suck moisture from the earth to a pulse so slow
you can't detect it. But my soul can read
the beat, and is looking for a new language
to translate the pleasure of this power.
It's tigress. Low tremendous purrs start at the pit
of my stomach, I'm curving through long grass,
all sinew, in a body where tension
is the special joy and where the half-second
before a leap tells it all. Put out a paw
to dab a stone, an ant, a dead lamb. Life,
my life, is all play even up to the moment
when I'm tripped up, thrown down, bound, raped until
I bleed from my eyes, beaten out of shape,
forced to bring forth war.

CAROL RUMENS
A BOOKSHOP REVISITED

(acknowledgements to Kingsley Amis and 'A Bookshop Idyll')

Between the NEW AGE and the FANTASY
    Comes more than one POETRY shelf.
By the lean Penguins, a Bloodaxe anthology
    Promotes itself.

Critical, though with plenty else to do,
    I scan the Contents Page,
Annoyed to find the names are mostly new
    And half my age.

Do titles offer clues to an author's sex?
    Lament for the Subotica Palic Tramway
Suggests a man, so do *Minus Three Point Six*
    And *Zoom* and *My Father at Fifty*.

From the Testament of the Reverend Thomas Dick,
    Very Simply Topping up the Brake Fluid,
To a Power Station, The Saltcoats Structuralists
    – I've got balls, I've got wheels. I've even read

Derrida, these titles bashfully say.
    But who'd have guessed *The Significance of Significance*
Shared an author with *The Graceful Giraffe of Clot Bey*?
    What about *Getting a Tan* or *Frog Prince*?

And who wrote *Hermaphroditus*? That's anyone's guess.
    If there's a story
Sometimes in titles, much here's genderless:
    Could that be its glory?

Women are often glad to be one of the crowd
    And not special cases.
But some would argue there's still a place for proud
    Self-proclaimed poetesses.

Should poetry editors bicycle-pump the issue
    Or squash it flat?
Is poetry made of moist erectile tissue
    Or not like that?

It's a good question, and I've pondered on it
    With Toril Moi,
Asking, each time I gave birth to a sonnet,
    "Is it a boy?"

Critical Theory is certainly a woman.
    She's French and exotic.
From *Langue et Parole* to *L'Écriture Feminine*,
    Mon Dieu, she's erotic!

Men write from a definite angle of masculinity.
    Will it never strike them?
Men are so chilling in their simplicity –
    Why on earth do we like them?

Poet or poetess, we've surely known times
    We sat up all night
In our Yeatsian masks, like good little androgynes,
    And couldn't write.

GRACE NICHOLS
MNEMOSYNE

(Greek Goddess of Memory)

It won't wash with me –
those who say you're a doddery old lady
dispensing bowls of maggoty soup
and mothy memoirs to all and sundry.
An unreliable witness in rose-coloured specs.

Oh no, you're as true as the saltbrine of the sea
to the emotional crystals –
not just the dotting of i's and crossing of t's.
The amnesiac, fish trapped in the mirrorless present,
wants nothing but to bring you flooding back –
all the driftwood, salt, lovehates and honey;
Mnemosyne, Memory, Mother of poetry.

Reprinted from Grace Nichols, *sunris* (Virago, 1996) by permission of
Curtis Brown Ltd.

CAROL ANN DUFFY
EURYDICE

Girls, I was dead and down
in the Underworld, a shade,
a shadow of my former self, nowhen.
It was a place where language stopped,
a black full-stop, a black hole
where words had to come to an end.
And end they did there,
last words,
famous or not.
It suited me down to the ground.

So imagine me there,
unavailable,
out of this world,
then picture my face in that place
of Eternal Repose,
in the one place you'd think a girl would be safe
from the kind of a man
who follows her round
writing poems,
hovers about
while she reads them,
calls her his Muse,
and once sulked for a night and a day
because she remarked on his weakness for abstract nouns;
just picture my face
when I heard –
Ye Gods –
a familiar knock-knock-knock at Death's door.

Him.
Big O.
Larger than life.
With his lyre
and a poem to read with me as the prize.

Things were different back then.
For the men, verse-wise,
Big O. was the boy.

Legendary. The blurb
on the back of his books claimed
that animals,
aardvark to zebra,
flocked to his side when he sang,
fish leapt from their waves
at the sound of his voice,
even the mute, sullen stones at his feet
wept wee silver tears.

Bollocks. Furthermore,
we've all, let's be honest,
been bored half to death by a man
who fucks like he's writing a book.
And, given my time all over again,
I know that I'd rather write for myself
than be dearest, beloved, dark lady, white goddess, etc. etc.

In fact, girls, I'd rather be dead.

But the Gods are like publishers –
usually male –
and what you doubtless know of my tale
is the deal.

Orpheus strutted his stuff.

The bloodless ghosts were in tears.
Sisyphus sat on his rock for the first time in years.
Tantalus was permitted a couple of beers.

The woman in question could scarcely believe her ears.

Like it or not,
I must follow him back to our life –
Eurydice, Orpheus's wife –
to be trapped in his images, metaphors, similes,
octaves and sextets, quatrains and couplets,
elegies, limericks, villanelles,
histories, myths . . .

I thought: *Sod this.*

He'd been told that he mustn't look back
or turn round,
but walk steadily upwards,
myself right behind him,
out of the Underworld
into the upper air that for me was the past.
He'd been warned
that one look would lose me
for ever and ever.

So onwards we walked.
Nobody talked.

Girls, forget what you've read,
it happened like this –
I did everything in my power
to make him look back.
What did I have to do, I said,
to make him see we were through?
I was *dead*. Deceased.
I was Resting in Peace. Passé.
Late. Past my sell-by date –
and here I stretched out my hand
and touched him once
on the back of the neck –
Please let me stay.
But already the light had saddened from purple to grey.

It was an uphill schlep
from death to life
and with every step
I willed him to turn.
I'd managed to filch the poem
out of his cloak
when inspiration finally struck.
I stopped, thrilled.
He was a yard in front.
My voice shook when I spoke –
Orpheus, your poem's a masterpiece.
I'd love to hear it again.

He was smiling modestly
when he turned
when he turned and he looked at me.

What else?
I noticed he hadn't shaved.
I waved once and was gone.

The dead are so talented.
The living walk by the edge of a vast lake
near the wise, drowned silence of the dead.

EVA SALZMAN
BARGAIN WITH THE WATCHMAN

There were two extra hooks of a worrying nature.
You'd better say it. We didn't know what we were doing.

The cratered earth, woven with roots, admitted nothing:
only later, when the pegs slid in, the canvas grew taut.

We'd browsed along the Cantal roads like butterflies,
settling lightly in a peaceful upland spot.

But the dogs barked in advance of the enemy,
the farmer riding shotgun on his tractor.

I had to strike a bargain with the watchman:
ten francs, some unwanted perfume and a burgundy kiss.

My shadow's length weighed me down like a lover,
a nightmare pressing: rose-lit arches, confetti or skin.

I was clutching the drooping tail of a pale horse
while you tethered the body, secured the spine.

Useless, I memorised the army-knife's position.
Then we drank their flaming water. Vichy.

JENNY JOSEPH
IN MEMORY OF PHILIP STONE

All over any small garden there are thousands
Of webs, of silk trails, the different formations
Of one or other out of a possible six hundred
Sorts of spider.   In Winter
Few are visible but they are there.

You may take your torch
Searching one spot, for a key dropped perhaps,
Or on a day when light strikes a dazzle of diamonds
From a thick wet hedge, get one whole and perfect
Made in a flash.

Spider silk is incredibly tough and spiders
Reconstitute at great speed to repair ruins.

Something in the clinging fuzz that repels
Our fingers, picking out from corners of drawers
A disgusting ball of dust,
Healed fevered wounds when they used to bandage with it.
This same coating it is preserves the web.

    Walking a short-cut path from the shops
    I hear crying behind a hedge
    (Run to see, pick the child up
    Find its Mum, take the child home?)
    Then round the corner comes
    The child held tight by its mother
    Still crying, still upset and angry
    But crying within the bounds of safety.

    Later the abysses of grief
    – Dismay like a river widening –
    Cannot be crossed by an arm round shaking shoulders.
    To grown children we cannot rush
    Encircle within our arms,
    Pick up, hold tight, console.

Something happens: snow falls
Or the fog blows back.
We are in another place than we had thought
And we see some things in the dark winter garden
We had not known were there.

The gossamer patches discovered with a new day
May have been there a very long time, as may the carcass
Of some animal that Autumn, night and winter
Snow-leaded weeks of dark   and fog
Hid, and whose habitation and progress through its life
We knew nothing of.

Those we love
We hold moments of, illuminations
Kept delicate and whole even when
The land is consigned to Winter and the dark,
And no one seems to go there, and there seems no movement
At all under the iron cold sky.

HELEN DUNMORE
FISHING BEYOND SUNSET

The boy in the boat, the tip of the pole,
slow swing of the boat as the wash goes round
from other boats with lights on, heading home
to islands, from islands: anyway they come.

Thirty-four bass, small bass, not worth keeping.
See them in the water, the hang
of twice-caught fish playing dumb,
then the shake-off of air. The kickdown

always surprises you, makes your feet grip
on the planks of the boat. There is the line
disappearing into the sunset
or so it seems, but it is plumbed

by your finger, which sees nothing
but a breeze of line running through water.
Behind you a sheet of fire
does something to pole, to boat, to boy.

U. A. FANTHORPE
POSTCARDS

(for Christine Wells)

The walkabout postman studies his handful
Before he slots them home. What do they say?

Public as T-shirts, coded like
A mole's correspondence, designed to be enigmatic.

Having a wonderful, they say. *Oh boy,*
This is the life! or *Cooler now. Had to put*

Our cardies on, they say, or *Natives friendly,*
Or just *Wish you were here.* He knows, the postman,

They don't say what they mean, mean what they say.
Extraordinary too, he thinks, the cards they send:

Of opera houses; owls; folk being ethnic;
Fish; teapots; *eucryphia milleganii*

(What'll she make of that? he thinks, popping it in.)
Each picture sends a message – proud, witty, pretty, wise –

But not enough for him to understand.
(*Super day yesterday sorry I missed the post.*)

O postman, postman, endlessly chivvied by cliché ,
This freakish correspondence that teases you so
Is a minor rehearsal for the final take-off.

Look in the graveyard, as you make your round;
There are the ultimate postcards, trite as ever,
Stylised as runes, with a subtext intricate

As a crossword puzzle clue, or house-agent's blurb,
Delivering the last message of stay-at-homes
To those who have left on a journey beyond deliveries:

Gone, not forgotten; Sadly missed; Wish you were here.

Sceptical Pressure

DENNIS O'DRISCOLL ON THE SELECTED POEMS OF THE WINNER OF
THE 1996 NOBEL PRIZE FOR LITERATURE

WISŁAWA SZYMBORSKA

View with a Grain of Sand:
Selected Poems

translated by Stanisław Barańczak and Clare Cavanagh
Faber, £8.99
ISBN 0 571 19163 0

CONDENSED WISDOM IS what Wisława Szymborska offers. Her poetry combines the deepest of insights with the lightest of touches; it is detached but not impersonal, ironic but not evasive, moral but not hectoring. To read her exemplary work is to feel a sudden surge of regret at the shallowness of so much contemporary poetry, at the premium increasingly placed on cleverness, at the predictability with which gender issues are handled. As Felicity Rosslyn has observed, Szymborska does not write "under political pressure or feminist pressure" but under "the pressure of her scepticism".

A slow coming she had of it. Even the Swedish Academy's Nobel citation spoke of "a handful of slim but powerful collections of poems"; and the earliest of these seem to have been composed with her hand stretched to the far left. Magnus J. Krynski and Robert A. Maguire, whose excellent translations of seventy Szymborska poems appeared in 1981, tactfully mentioned the "officially inspired themes" of the early books, while Piotr Sommer recently alluded to "two early (collections) she prefers to forget about". Reviewing the American edition of *View with a Grain of Sand*, which appeared last year, Edward Hirsch referred more specifically to poems which "range from dogmatic denunciations of the old order to strident condemnations of Western imperialism". Fortunately, Szymborska overcame her initial conformism to become the most independent of poets; and if her career began far less strikingly than that of her coura-

geous contemporary, Zbigniew Herbert, she gradually accumulated a body of work so consistently strong that it could stand comparison with his.

View with a Grain of Sand, like the bilingual Krynski/Maguire volume, takes as its starting-point Szymborska's third collection, *Calling Out to Yeti*, published in 1957 when she was thirty-four. With each collection, her wit quickens, her gaze widens, her scepticism sharpens. Far less politically-minded than Herbert though she may be, she is nonetheless conscious of the pervasiveness of politics ("All day long, all through the night, / all affairs – yours, ours, theirs – / are political affairs".); and the weight she attached, when the prevailing ethos was collectivist, to the fate of the individual ("my imagination ... is bad with large numbers. / It's still taken by particularity".) is not without political implications. Her poems are paradigms of freedom, spaces in which assumptions are subtly challenged and orthodoxies quietly subverted. Hers is a poetry of the ordinary: her average day is so mundane as to be forgettable ("One of those many dates / that no longer ring a bell"); no one in her family "has ever died of love. / No food for myth and nothing magisterial".

A poet of enormously diverse subject-matter, Szymborska derives some of her "springboards for the spirit" from extensive reading of non-literary books for review; as with Marianne Moore, the natural world is a favourite source. An endangered sea-cucumber dividing itself in two prompts a deeply-moving elegy ("Life on one shore, death on the other"); another poem inspects mankind through the huge eyes of a tarsier. Humans, to whom she denies supremacy over nature, are viewed by Szymborska with an amalgam of bemusement and horror; no poet could be less deceived – and yet her tone is more often exuberant than downcast. Perhaps, like Patrick Kavanagh, she senses that – in art at least – "Tragedy is underdeveloped Comedy":

For me the tragedy's most important act is the sixth:
the raising of the dead from the stage's battlegrounds,
the straightening of wigs and fancy gowns,
removing knives from stricken breasts,
taking nooses from lifeless necks,
lining up among the living
to face the audience.

It is not only the inexhaustible variety of Szymborska's subject-matter (from a medieval miniature to a mathematical symbol) and the entertaining ingenuity with which she presents it (using a CV, a spoof critique, an overheard conversation, for example) that are impressive but the extent to which her "essay-poems" prove to be both crisp and comprehensive. Although different in almost every other respect from Czeslaw Milosz, she shares with him the uncanny ability to see things *sub specie aeternitatis*, to simultaneously inhabit and transcend time.

It is regrettable that, in the wake of Szymborska's unexpected but certainly not undeserved Nobel Prize, Faber have merely rushed out the American edition of *View with a Grain of Sand*, which lamentably lacks any introduction or background notes. Happily, however, the translations by Barańczak and Cavanagh are admirably supple, taking tricky puns and rhymes in their stride; and her poems are distilled into English which – shimmering as dew, transparent as water, potent as alcohol – honours her aspiration that everything she writes should seem intelligible and clear. There ought to be a vodka called Szymborska.

Taken by Particularity

SZYMBORSKA – JERZY JARNIEWICZ GIVES THE OPINION POLSKA

WHEN THE NEWS of this year's Nobel Prize reached Poland, Wisława Szymborska was, characteristically, in a retreat in the Tatra Mountains. Seamus Heaney, visiting Cracow at that time, paid her a tribute during his literary evening by reading one of her poems translated into English by another Nobel Prize winner, Joseph Brodsky. In this way the three Nobel poets held an unexpected symbolic meeting in the former capital of Poland. When on this occasion one of the journalists asked me to compare this year's and last year's winners, the thing that instantly came to mind was that whereas Heaney is an exquisite myth-builder, Szymborska is a declared destroyer of myths.

With the precision of a surgeon, and with the surgeon's paramount tranquillity, she cuts deep into the trunks of dogmas, conventions and stereotypes. It is an astonishing blend of the surgical compulsion to demythologise, and the classical, some would say "Mozartian", elegance with which she performs her dissections.

Hers is a poetry of wide perspectives, historical, or evolutionary; a backdrop against which human ambitions, as well as human frustrations, can best be measured. In this way, Szymborska manages to avoid the dangers of topicality and localism which burden so much of modern Polish poetry. It is her great achievement that she does not gain this universality at the cost of losing sight of the details, even if it were only "a grain of sand". On the contrary, her wide perspectives would not exist without everyday trivia, and the poet admits her imagination is "taken by particularities". Thus Szymborska's work is balanced between "the time of insects" and "the time of stars", remaining attentive to both, though preferring the former. When she observes a newly discovered star, she sees it is "between that gray cloud's jagged edge and the acacia twig over there on the left".

The secret of Szymborska's unique ability to unmask false assumptions lies in what some would call "methodological doubt", others – wilful naivety, though not so much in its amazement at the wonders of the world, as in its readiness to pose even the simplest questions ("the most pressing questions are naive ones"). In the 1950's Szymborska passed through a short period of infatuation with Marxism and the crude socialist-realism doctrine. This experience has made her very cautious about any dogmatic systems, even those, and perhaps especially those, which promise the amelioration of the human lot and which prefer "mankind to people". Since then she has discovered the recuperative value of doubt, which she has happily married to her inimitable irony and humour.

And yet her refusal to take anything for granted has not carried her into the cul-de-sac of nihilism. In her poetry Szymborska tries to retrieve that which is marginalized or suppressed by the impersonal processes of history, by ideology or art, in fact, by any usurpative act of thoughtless generalisation. She inquires about the "skinny sisters" of Rubens' women, who had been "exiled by style". Dissatisfied with the official version of Lot's story, she compiles a long list of reasons for which Lot's wife looked back – apart from the supposed curiosity. In an ironic way Szymborska recaptures the wonders of the world in what is most common, simple and ordinary. A sense of wonder always accompanies her demythologising insights.

Her poetry avoids giving answers, concerning itself with something more important: the opening of doors to further questions and inquiries. Her poems are often personal dialogues which the poet conducts with herself, or emotional debates with received ideas and commonplaces. Some are composed almost entirely of questions. Some develop in a sequence of statements which are, simultaneously, modified, or refuted. "How many of those I knew / (if I really knew them), / men, women / (if the distinction still holds) / have crossed that threshold / (if it is a threshold) / passed over that bridge / (if you can call it a bridge)". Reality is too various to be encapsulated in any single truth.

Yet though these polyphonic compositions deconstruct, question and complicate truths taken for granted, the result is, paradoxically, a feeling of greater clarity and order. The poet has somehow managed to domesticate chaos, without simplifying it. Her irony and humour, saving the poems from the traps of nihilism, show that it is not the poet who is at the mercy of the demythologised truths, it is these truths which are in the hands of the less deceived poet. Inevitably, one could say, her poetry proclaims the sovereignty of the individual and the belief in "the possibility that existence has its own reason for being".

Szymborska's distrust of all systems shapes her attitude towards the feminist issue. She has denounced the feminist label: "I think that the divisions into women's poetry and men's poetry are becoming absurd. Today there is nothing which would not concern both women and men. We do not live in a boudoir any longer". Although she has written a few poems which deal specifically with the condition of women, she undermines all the clichés about so-called women's poetry. Her intellectual, reserved poetry is thus a safeguard against any kind of stereotype, no matter from which side of the barricade it comes. Steering clear of the stereotypical "feminine" traits, Szymborska, more than many other women poets, extends the territory of contemporary women's writing.

Her classical qualities, which make her stand apart, but never aloof, from literary or political coteries, do not mean that she has adopted a detached olympian stance. Without compromising her art and her sovereignty, she responded to the nightmarish reality of martial law in Poland in such poems as 'An Opinion on the Question of Pornography'. Several years ago, when the country was in danger of falling prey to mad ambitions of nationalistic, populist politicians, one of the greatest Polish newspapers published Szymborska's poem, 'Hatred', on its front page. The next time Szymborska's poems appeared on the front pages of the newspapers was in October 1996.

WISŁAWA SZYMBORSKA
NOTHING TWICE

Nothing can ever happen twice.
In consequence, the sorry fact is
that we arrive here improvised
and leave without the chance to practice.

Even if there is no one dumber,
if you're the planet's biggest dunce,
you can't repeat the class in summer:
this course is only offered once.

No day copies yesterday,
no two nights will teach what bliss is
in precisely the same way,
with exactly the same kisses.

One day, perhaps, some idle tongue
mentions your name by accident:
I feel as if a rose were flung
into the room, all hue and scent.

The next day, though you're here with me,
I can't help looking at the clock:
A rose? A rose? What could that be?
Is it a flower or a rock?

Why do we treat the fleeting day
with so much needless fear and sorrow?
It's in its nature not to stay:
Today is always gone tomorrow.

With smiles and kisses, we prefer
to seek accord beneath our star,
although we're different (we concur)
just as two drops of water are.

TRANSLATED BY STANISŁAW BARAŃCZAK
AND CLARE CAVANAGH

Reprinted from Wisława Szymborska, *View With a Grain
of Sand*, by permission of Faber & Faber.

NEW POETS '97

JANE HOLLAND

I WAS BORN in Ilford in 1966 but moved to the Isle of Man with my family in 1977. My mother is a novelist and my father a retired journalist, so from an early age I was surrounded by literature. I married at nineteen, abandoning any thought of a career in order to raise a family. Then in 1990 I started playing snooker on the ladies' world circuit. This became full-time quite rapidly, my highest ranking being 24th in the world. Following an argument with the local snooker committee in late 1994, I was banned indefinitely on the charge of "bringing the game into disrepute". I lost my faith in the sport and decided to try something completely different. So I started writing poetry. At that time, the only living poet I had heard of was Ted Hughes! To educate myself, I founded *Blade* in 1995, a poetry magazine which publishes British and American poetry and reviews, plus poetry in translation. Over the past year, I have had work accepted by various magazines, including *PN Review*, *London Magazine*, *The Rialto*, *Iron* and *The North*. Much to my surprise, I won an Eric Gregory in 1996, and my first collection, *The Brief History of a Disreputable Woman*, will be published by Bloodaxe later this year.

LOCO

There is a train,
an endless track of railroad in my head.

The tracks are over-run with seed,
they clamour with the scent of grass.

Beneath the bridge,
an arch of moss has taken hold.

The flags are up.
The whistle blows – 3.30 every day

a ritual of steam and speed
and racing wind.

I fashioned you from singing-steel.
I hammered out a ring

that cooled in locomotive style.
I took your breath,

your cold indifference
and blew it through a tunnel

like an iron god –
the shriek, the whistle in the dark!

I am all talk,
all track.

I sway as grass
green-bent on gravel in the heat,

the fire of your passing,
steam-blown-white, unstoppable.

THE NEWEL-POST

Where her passing hand had always touched.
Where the feet of generations pause
for wood, white-washed, under their fingers.

Up there, below the eaves, brushing stiffly
against shadows at the top of the stairs,
there is a music in the creaking boards.

It comes like rain, tapping out its rhythm
in darkness, a blind man with a stick.
I wait for the inevitable hand, welcome it.

Once, she was there for a whole evening,
sitting on her own with the hall-light off.
I think I might have heard her crying

but it could just have been the cat, lashing
her long black tail around my frame.
She played that message again and again.

At night, I am a magnet for moonlight.
I count myself to the tick of the clock.
Upstairs, somebody wakes, coughs softly.

I will keep awake for them: alert
to the brisk feet of whistling milkmen,
the newspaper thud, a slither of post.

She never seems to see me, though I watch her
sometimes when she leaves the door ajar,
the kettle on, my painted surface steaming.

I recognise her by her changing tread.
I am that point along the passageway
where flesh and spirit tremble into wood.

THEY ARE A TABLEAU
AT THE KISSING-GATE

Maids of honour, bridegroom, bride,
the best man in a grey silk suit,
a flash to catch them in the arching
stone, confettied by a sudden gust –
an apple-tree in full white spread
beyond the reach of bone and dust.

I am the driver in a passing car:
the wedding-dress a cloud of lace.
A small hand clutching at a skirt,
some nervous bridesmaid, eight
or maybe nine years old, has seen
the blossom fall, has closed her eyes –

her head falls back into the scent,
the soundless whirr and whirl of earth-
bound petals, like sycamore seeds
on a current of air, silent helicopters
bringing light – a wedding-gift
the bride will brush away, unconsciously.

This is no ordinary act, no summer fête,
another simple wedding held in June.
This is the wind shaking the apple-tree,
the bell above the kissing-gate,
the sudden fall of blossom into light
which only love and innocence can see.

We must be held accountable to love:
where they step out together arm in arm
as newly-weds, spring-cleaned, and climb
into a waiting car beneath a summer sky,
the blossom will still fall, unstoppable –
a drift of change across a changeless time.

A SECOND LOOK

Downhill, Mad as Swine

JOHN HARTLEY WILLIAMS ON THE POETRY OF ROSEMARY TONKS

"Poets are only at work,
With an agate daylight going through the street,
When they live, dream, *bleed*,– within an inch of
giving in to art".
– Rosemary Tonks, 'April and the Ideas Merchant'

IF EVER THERE was a low, dishonest decade, it was the sixties. It began, approximately speaking, with an affair that was ostensibly about national security but which was really a nasty affair of national prudery and voyeurism in which a man called Stephen Ward was hounded to suicide for having an interesting sex life. It ended, again rather approximately, but very spectacularly, with a student revolt in France that some people saw as Surrealism finally taking to the barricades ("Choose life instead"). This provoked the usual sort of Edmund Burke noises in Britain ("We don't want any of that *here*") and a strict ban on radical student agitators from France entering the country. (In the European Union of now that might be a little harder to achieve, though I can already imagine the glint of foam on Michael Howard's lips.) What we had then in Britain was the swinging sixties (actually an invention of *Time* magazine), and pop music. Four lovable, tousle-headed youngsters wrote effortlessly trite ditties that, even today, no matter how you turn your radio dial, just won't go away. No doubt about it, we had a thinning of our dream diet to the point where a kind of anorexia of the imagination took over.

We also had "poetry" (of a sort). The word acquired a sort of heroic meaninglessness. Everybody wanted to be thought of as a "poet" – the rock guitarists, the fashion designers, the hit parade lyricists. What we had was "poetry in motion" – which was Julie Christie swanning

> She's a proto-punk minxette,
> rising from the bourgeois ashes
> of family and home
> seeking "heavenly spoil".

through some northern city at the beginning of the film *Billy Liar*. "Poetry" was sexy, it made money, it was beautiful people doing wonderfully inconsequential things. Above all, it was being in the newspapers – what Rosemary Tonks called the "pork newspapers" – so we had the "poetry" of tennis-players, of architects, of kings and queens, hairdressers, club owners and superlatively crooked financiers. The poetry of poets very soon lost so much currency that by the time the seventies came around, poets started to read books on linguistics and call their poems "texts". Just as the "poetry" the "pork newspapers" discovered everywhere seemed replete with spirituality, discernment, intellectuality, catholicity of expression and what have you (you knew immediately which tennis players they were talking about) the real poets started putting a line through anything they'd written that smacked of spirituality, discernment, intellectuality, catholicity of expression etc. etc. What else could they do?

That this cultural hyperbole began in the sixties, I take as axiomatic. In an environment like that there was not much else a poet could do but "live, dream, *bleed* – within an inch of giving in to art". One might add "within an inch of giving in to the media" as well. Thoughts such as these, or grunts rather, are occasioned by re-reading the work of Rosemary Tonks, who published two books of poetry in the sixties, and had her epoch down to a T:

I understand you, frightful epoch,
With your jampots, brothels, paranoias,
And your genius for fear, you can't stop shuddering.
Discotheques, I drown among your husky broken
sentences.
('Epoch of the Hotel Corridor')

Poets, of course, as we all know, are either of their time or for all time. Rosemary Tonks was both. She wasn't just a poet *of* the sixties – she was a true poet of any era – but she has sent us strange messages from them, alive, fresh and surprising today as the *anni domini* they were minted in were glum. She descends deep inside herself to where humour really starts, draws up what she finds there, and releases it with an apparent casualness, yet gritting her teeth as she does so. She directs lampoon-boomerangs of contempt at the edifices of rectitude and cliché all around her, hears them clonk satisfyingly, catches them on their return and sends them spinning off again in a new and startling direction. What you meet in her poems is a personality of revolutionary sulkiness, of outraged and witty petulance, mulling mutinously, mock-pedantically over her revolt:

> Inquire of my ability to be last off the streets
> When I am molten, stupid, dangerous,
> Under an alley's aspic wall with bullying confederates
> In arms, love, lies, and law-breakings.
> And for my knowledge of the dawn
> Examine me upon the solitary power-drunk return

> From the nocturnal city

That comes from a poem called 'Apprentice'. It appeared in her first book, published in 1963 by Putnam, called *Notes on Cafés and Bedrooms*. Her second book, *Iliad of Broken Sentences*, was published by The Bodley Head in 1967. Neither of these books has been reprinted and rumour has it that the poet, like Rimbaud, has turned her back on them, yet there is possibly no other poet who has caught with such haughty, self-ironising contempt, the loucheness of the period, or the anger it could touch off in brooding bystanders. The poem 'Apprentice' toys hoydenishly with the idea of an abandonment to the educational process that would "tame with toolbag or certificate / My shudder". The challenge of: "Inquire", "Examine me", "Test me", however, contain the implied riposte: it won't do you much good. Here we find the typical Tonks roster of adjectives – the "aspic" wall, the "bullying" confederates, the "power-drunk" return – all of which seem to imply a kind of contradiction. She assumes guises, personalities: "When I am molten, stupid, dangerous". She's a proto-punk minxette, rising from the bourgeois ashes of family and home seeking "heavenly spoil". It's as a "gloveless trespasser" that she "desires supremacy". The word "gloveless" captures

exactly her desire of "not giving in to art". In a poem from her second book that same refusal to give in, this time to life, is expressed as follows:

> Meanwhile … I live on … powerful, disobedient,
> Inside their draughty haberdasher's climate,
> With these people … who are going to obsess me,
> Potatoes, dentists, people I hardly know, it's
>   unforgivable
> For this is not my life
> But theirs, that I am living.
> And I wolf, bolt, gulp it down, day after day.
>   ('Addiction To An Old Mattress')

This extract reflects another Tonks characteristic, the use of dashes (dots, actually) as a rhythmic and syntactic device. (Nothing like Emily Dickinson, therefore.) What gives the lines their undated freshness is the way they catch the speaking voice, its unfinished sentences, its breaks and hiatuses, its dying falls. The lines are rhythmical and repetitive, as speech is, shot through with interjections, contradictions and self-parodying assertions. This is from 'Song of the October Wind' (also from her second book):

> At home,

> My sofa wrote her creaking, narcoleptic's Iliad.
> My bathroom drank the Styx (bathwater
> Of the Underworld). My telephone took all its voices
> And gave them to the Furies, to practise with.

> While slowly – to gigantic, muddy blows of music
> From a pestle and mortar – roof, floor, walls, doors,
> My London, stuffed with whisky-dark hotels,
> Began to pant like a great ode!

The delicate preposterousness of this is irresistible. It's alarming, exuberant, angry, and very very funny. The metropolis – lovingly and loathingly described – is where most of her poems are set. Railway stations, cafés, alien rooms are her chosen locations, but they may turn out to be completely elsewhere – Asia, Istanbul, or whatever. The sense of wilful exile is very strong. When she takes a train to the seaside, for example, she imagines herself in a plasterboard hotel bedroom, lying musing, interlocked with her lover, as they sink to a vast depth: "Like deportees who undulate to phosphorescent booming". Or else, of course, her poems are set in Kurdistan (or any part of Arabia Deserta you care to imagine). "Correct your maps: Newcastle is Peru", said John Cleveland. Tonks relocates London in "Europe's old blue Kasbah". She's a "Bedouin of the London evening" who loses her youth on the way to a restaurant. The awful, catastrophic hilarity of what happens to her in no way mitigates the Olympian non-detachment with which she contemplates it:

We were the young, derisive metropolitans
Soon to be mashed flat as a wet coalsack by skies
Of ochre

('Fog Peacocks')

A journey across London on an ordinary double-decker ('An Old-Fashioned Traveller on the Trade Routes') is both Biblical (the travellers are "flung about softly like trusses of wheat") and zoological (the bus itself becomes an eminent jellyfish propelling itself 'with an iron will, by expulsions, valves, hisses, steams, and emotional respirations'). She writes of lovers and of love with a kind of elegiac disgust: "He's timid with women and the dusk is excruciating". When lovers embrace it is with an "enlightened coarseness". She's not disillusioned; she simply has no illusions: "Isn't there always / The unreliability, the cool mouth-bite of a beloved body?" The erotic unease that pervades much of the poems seesaws between the chance for a loathed surrender, and the possibilities of a longed-for rejection. She imagines herself (post-coitally, perhaps) at a solitary table in a restaurant "where we end up / At the mercy of a salt and pepper pot", and concludes:

One wound from Eros
And your breast can only drink arrows

With its illiterate and fragrant mud,
(Teetotaler, dead drunk on your own blood.)
It's ludicrous! It's hopeless.
Shut up your underworlds! Close your hearts!

The century is over. Doors are slamming
In the tragic, casual era. The Eros of dead café tunes
Is in your voice . . .
He salts and peppers me another pair of arms.

('To A Certain Young Man')

If that isn't a brilliant way to end a poem, I don't know what is. Rosemary Tonks' imagery has a daring for which it's hard to find a parallel in British poetry. Too much of what we are offered to read

these days is poetry of the head. Craftsy and artsy, it attempts to forestall criticism with its cleverness. As Roy Campbell memorably said: "They use the snaffle and the curb all right, / But where's the bloody horse?". What we have is *occasional* poetry by the bucketful. On the other hand, our would-be bareback riders exhibit what André Breton described as "the carelessness of the vast majority of authors who [are] generally content to let their pens run rampant over the paper without making the least effort to observe what [is] going on inside themselves". He added: "we still know as little as we ever did about the origin of that voice which it is everyone's prerogative to hear, if only he will, a voice which converses with us most specifically about something other than what we believe we are thinking, and upon occasion assumes a serious tone when we feel most light-hearted or deals in idle prattle when we are unhappiest". It's that attentiveness to what is really going on inside herself which gives Rosemary Tonks' poetry its vitality – attentiveness to that voice whose conversation seems to be continually surprising itself. Her imagery is full of upsurging unconscious power:

Now for the night, liquid or bristling!
When owls make the ink squeak at my window
And my bedroom that can bone my body of its will,
Drinks out my brain on pillows.

('The Solitary's Bedroom')

Most of all, it's the sense of revolt which makes these poems live. Key words are brown, caked, crusted, mud, fog, dead, cabbage stumps, dust-drowned, green, greenish-yellow. London is bronze-brown and half-lit, a deep bronze, filled with wind and dust, an "Imperial rubbish heap of wastrels, scullions, houris, fauns, and bedouin", and she cries out against it all: "Tradesmen, pigs, regenerative trains – I shall be saved!". There's much of the feeling of Rimbaud's "Les poëtes de sept ans" in all of this. In a poem called 'The Sash Window' she describes the "hellish, abominable house where I have been young". She remembers the window with its "servant-maid's mystery, which contains *nothing*" where she:

bowed over the ruled-up music books
With their vitreous pencilling, and the piano keys
That touched water. How forlornly my strong,
destructive head
Eats again the reek of the sash window.

The description of one of those suburban London houses with its –

> insane furnishings – above all
> The backs of dressing-tables where the dredged wood
> Faces the street, raw.

– has you noting the acerbic and haughty precision of that adjective "dredged". That sense of rebellion and disgust, combined with a kind of lunatic acquiescence, runs unabatedly through all the poems. And of course it's the tone that strikes you, seeming to come from somewhere French, through Laforgue, perhaps, with a little of Nerval, a touch of German expressionism, Gottfried Benn perhaps? (I'm thinking of his poem 'D-Zug', which begins with a litany of colours, like a Tonks poem: "Braun wie Kognak, Braun wie Laub, Rotbraun, Malaiengelb / D-Zug Berlin-Trelleborg und die Ostseebäder". Compare, from 'Farewell to Kurdistan': "The railway sheds are full of greenish-yellow electricity, / It's the great mid-day hour in London . . . that suddenly goes brown").

In her second and last book, there is a poem called 'Dressing Gown Olympian' which begins like this:

> I insist on vegetating here
> In moth eaten grandeur. Haven't I plotted
> Like a madman to get here? Well then.

Well then, indeed. The sixties were a period of post-Imperial illusion, a débâcle whose grotesque and importunate tactics have somehow continued to dominate British cultural and political life without actually finding any kind of conclusion, any kind of dialectical exit. What makes the poetry of Rosemary Tonks special is that it contemptuously dispenses with tactics. She made *her* exit, it's true, but there's something admirably Rimbaudian about that. These days a belief seems to have grown up that poets can have a "career". The skillful poetaster can usually manipulate himself (or herself) a seat on the board of Art and Culture plc. Poetry can even be marketed as rock 'n' roll, but no semi-ironic disclaimers of such activity for and on behalf of the publicity machine will discharge poets from their responsibility for exercising the freedom of their imaginations. And there's no point in pretending the real audience for poetry will ever be other than the poet's friends.

In Rosemary Tonks' two books you will find a freedom, a wonderful extravagance, a strangeness and a seriousness that is rare in English poetry. I am not even going to suggest they should be republished. Friends will know where to look for them. In 1968, French students scrawled André Breton's final sentence to his book *Nadja*: "Beauty will be convulsive or will not be at all" on half the walls of Paris. For a moment, you could believe that, convulsively, beauty would *be*. When did Rosemary Tonks stop writing poems? We don't know. Why did she stop writing poems? We don't know that either. Of course, any kind of violent cultural action underwrites its own demise. Poems, on the other hand, must stop when they reach the brink of art, or become assimilated. It's a very complex state of affairs. Incidentally, a postscript to that dreadful decade (whose intestate legacy we are still paying off) was written by Jean Schuster, head of the Surrealist movement after the death of André Breton, on February 8th 1969. He disbanded the movement once and for all.

Select Bibliography

Notes on Cafés and Bedrooms (Putnam, 1963).
Iliad of Broken Sentences (The Bodley Head, 1967).

Courting the risk of John Hartley Williams' disapproval, Bloodaxe wish to publish a collected Rosemary Tonks in the near future and are appealing for her to contact them: Neil Astley, Bloodaxe Books, PO Box 1SN, Newcastle upon Tyne NE99 1SN.

THE CLASSIC POEM

1. SELECTED BY HERMIONE LEE

I LIKE POETRY as a weapon – tough, disabused poems, poems written by the less deceived, which savage pretensions, complacency, tyranny or sentiment. I like the mocking energy, the glee, and the severity, of poems such as Swift's 'Verses on the Death of Dr Swift' ("I love my friend as well as you / but would not have him stop my view"), or Shelley's 'Ozymandias', or Browning's 'Fra Lippo Lippi'. I would start an imaginary anthology of great twentieth century fierce poems with Larkin's 'Vers de Société', Stevie Smith's 'The Weak Monk' and 'Scorpion', James Fenton's 'The Mistake', Peter Reading's 'Final Demands', and Kit Wright's 'An Ill Wind': "nothing in his life having disinclined him from the view / that those who lose on the swings are likely to lose even more / on the roundabouts". That's not unlike the theme of my favourite fierce poem, Robert Frost's 'Provide, Provide', written in 1934 when the poet was sixty, a wonderfully ruthless meditation on the very American theme of winning and losing. Randall Jarrell in *Poetry and the Age*, brilliantly resurrecting Frost in the 1950s from a comfortable grave of sugary homeyness, called it "an immortal masterpiece", and he's right. He also called it "a *reductio ad absurdum* of expediency", which suggests that expediency, the "Wisdom of the World", in the end won't do: we may, after all, need to choose morality instead: "being simply true". I read 'Provide, Provide' less forgivingly. I don't think it gives much force to relying on "what you knew" or "being simply true"; I think it devastatingly tells you that you will need to plot for your survival or you'll go under. The coldly furious and ironic imperatives, the laconic neat 3-line rhymes, the tacky ordinariness of the "real life" references mixed with words that open out into a graver, more prophetic tone ("predestined", "disregard", "dignified", "boughten", and especially the biblical name Abishag) make the poem at once icy, sharp, deep and haunting. It is terribly dry, and terribly sad.

ROBERT FROST

PROVIDE, PROVIDE

The witch that came (the withered hag)
To wash the steps with pail and rag
Was once the beauty Abishag,

The picture pride of Hollywood.
Too many fall from great and good
For you to doubt the likelihood.

Die early and avoid the fate.
Or if predestined to die late,
Make up your mind to die in state.

Make the whole stock exchange your own!
If need be occupy a throne,
Where nobody can call *you* crone.

Some have relied on what they knew,
Others on being simply true.
What worked for them might work for you.

No memory of having starred
Atones for later disregard
Or keeps the end from being hard.

Better to go down dignified
With boughten friendship at your side
Than none at all. Provide, provide!

Reprinted from *The Poetry of Robert Frost*, ed. Edward Connery Lathem, by permission of the Estate of Robert Frost and Jonathan Cape Ltd.

2. SELECTED BY ELAINE FEINSTEIN

LOUISE GLÜCK IS a very fine American poet whose lyric intensity I have admired for many years. This poem is chosen from a recent collection, which takes the enormous gamble of finding human resonance in the life of plants. In 'The Wild Iris', the title poem, Gluck casually enters the consciousness of a bulb and speaks in the person of a flower, which is a risk of some magnitude. Her quiet voice has such authority, however, that for some time after reading these verses I was haunted by a sense of continuity between the living and the dead. It is not so easy to analyse how the poem achieves this. Her use of pace and pause is a part of it, certainly; for instance, in the gap between the first and second verse she allows scepticism and resistance to rise in us before silencing both with a command to listen. The language is literal, the only metaphor the central image, the act of imagination that of remembering burial, rather than fearing it. Her propositions, strange as they are, have an unforced directness and concision. Yet she makes us feel the deep blue fountain of the flower arising from the centre of its being like a voice.

LOUISE GLÜCK

THE WILD IRIS

At the end of my suffering
there was a door.

Hear me out: that which you call death
I remember.

Overhead, noises, branches of the pine shifting.
Then nothing. The weak sun
flickered over the dry surface.

It is terrible to survive
as consciousness
buried in the dark earth.

Then it was over: that which you fear, being
a soul and unable
to speak, ending abruptly, the stiff earth
bending a little. And what I took to be
birds darting in low shrubs.

You who do not remember
passage from the other world
I tell you I could speak again: whatever
returns from oblivion returns
to find a voice:

from the center of my life came
a great fountain, deep blue
shadows on azure seawater.

Reprinted from Louise Glück, *The Wild Iris*, by permission of Carcanet Press.

THE REVIEW PAGES

Bare and Frondish

HELEN DUNMORE FINDS, IN ANNE STEVENSON'S POETRY,
"AN ELUSIVE QUALITY OF WILDNESS, UNTAMED BUT NEVER CHAOTIC"

ANNE STEVENSON

The Collected Poems 1955–1995

Oxford Poets, £11.99
ISBN 0192832514

ANNE STEVENSON'S *Collected Poems* bring together the work of more than forty years. It is interesting to go back to the beginning of that period, and look at the world in which Anne Stevenson began to write.

It is 1955. The cold war grips Europe and America, and the Rosenbergs have been put to death as spies. England is said to be entering a new Elizabethan age, following the coronation of Queen Elizabeth II in 1953, though it is hard to tell quite what is meant by this. Women's clothes are changing: the clipped, square-shouldered outline of austerity has been challenged by long full skirts and nipped waists. The wartime mobilisation of women into employment and the armed forces has been deliberately reversed, and successful marriage and domesticity are put forward as the goals of all women, even the most highly educated. A young American woman, born in Grantchester, Cambridge, is writing poems. Another young American woman, born in New England, is about to cross the Atlantic and go to Cambridge on a Fulbright scholarship. She, too, is writing poems.

In looking at the past, we also revise it, and Anne Stevenson is candid about her decision to revise or to omit poems in the course of preparing this *Collected Poems*. In an interview with Richard Poole, published in *Poetry Wales* (Vol. 31, No 4) she comments on the cuts she has chosen to make to a poem called 'England'. "I wanted to retain it, but I had to chop some embarrassing bits out". A little later on she quotes Valéry's remark that "a poem is never finished, only abandoned". This remark of Valéry's was also quoted by Auden,

another thorough reviser of his earlier self.

The older poet looking back on his or her young self may be embarrassed or irritated by what she sees as gaucherie, clumsiness, or even pretentiousness. The desire to destroy or to rewrite the past is almost irresistible. Most of us do it through the unconscious manipulation of memory. Poets, seeing their inner life solidified and exposed on white pages, may well wish to change it in the light of later experience. But while we gain with age, we also lose. There are poems written at twenty-five which are beyond the writer of fifty. While Anne Stevenson is firm in her assertion of the right to change a poem, it may be that the flawed, embarrassing whole would be richer than she imagines.

What Stevenson offers is rich enough. Her scrutiny of the world in which she finds herself is witty, honest, precise and deeply humane. She is a magnificent poet of landscape. She is technically strong, with a particularly sure-footed sense of stress. Her responsiveness to changing times, to changing faces, to the unreeling of her own life, has an impressive clarity and lack of self-pity. And beyond all this there is an elusive quality of wildness, untamed but never chaotic, which makes her such a fine observer of the wildness in the world around: "Buzzard that folds itself into and becomes nude / alder, alder that insensibly becomes bird – / one life inside the dazzling tree". This kind of wildness is both self-sufficient and an integral part of a natural system.

Anne Stevenson's scrutinies of nature allow the poet to be absorbed by what she writes about, without trying to absorb it. She has the gift of letting things be themselves. 'Himalayan Balsam' moves from a perfect, sensuous evocation of the flowers: "Orchard-lipped, loose-jointed, purplish, indolent flowers, / with a ripe smell of peaches, like a girl's breath through lipstick . . ." to a meditation on the flowers "important descent" to disintegration in the river-bed. Stevenson remarks in parenthesis that "(I am combing abundant leaves from these icy shallows.)", but she continues to comb, in this poem driven by hunger for fleeting things, flowers, smells, embryo birds. The poem understands how necessarily as well as irrevocably death is knitted into the system.

Anne Stevenson's biography of Sylvia Plath, *Bitter Fame*, has its after-echo here in three poems for Sylvia Plath. It is hard enough for poets not to compare their own success with that of their contemporaries; almost impossible when one achieves sudden fame before another. Plath seems to have felt shaken by the early success of Adrienne Rich. Anne Stevenson began to publish when Plath was already dead and beginning to turn into a figure who might throw a colossal shadow over another woman poet of the same age and nationality. The poems Stevenson writes for Plath are constricted things in comparison with the fluid loveliness of the poems she writes to honour the memory of the poet Frances Horovitz. When writing of Plath, Stevenson cannot avoid impatience, and in the lines "Because you were selfish and sad and died" she seems to ignore the ravages of clinical, suicidal depression at a time when treatment was at best crude, at worst horrific. There is an unbecoming element of judgement in 'Letter to Sylvia Plath (Grantchester, May 1988)', even though it contains one stanza of masterly lyricism. Perhaps these two poets were too different ever to understand each other fully: Plath, so often ricocheting between the role of schooled, good girl and the company of her own rage; Stevenson, stepping aside from the very idea of a role with the fastidiousness of a cat.

Anne Stevenson is also cat-like in her sensuous responsiveness and ability to make her imagination at home as she moves from place to place. She is capable of an intense stillness, in which she gathers intelligence and brings it home to change into the substance of a poem. She seems to get to the heart

of place very quickly, rather as D. H. Lawrence did, and there is something of Lawrence in her understanding of structure, whether that of a plant, a landscape or a local society. In her poem 'A Prayer to Live with Real People' she notes not only the "sweet sixteen-stone ladies, / luscious as pom-poms or full blown perfumed magnolias, / breasts like cottage loaves dropped into lace-knit sweaters", but also "the tattooed forearm steering the cue like a pencil". It is that "steering" which shows the quality of Stevenson's perceptions and their translation into language. The simile floats easily on its backwash. This is inhabited poetry, as Stevenson defines it in her 'Making Poetry': "To be in the habit of, to wear / words, sitting in the plainest light, / in the silk of morning, in the shoe of night, / a feeling bare and frondish in surprising air; / familiar . . . rare".

Her feeling for the topography of the landscapes she inhabits is acute. These are maps made by feet testing the contours and hands touching them. They explore America, England, Scotland, Wales. Stevenson has cottages in Grantchester and in Cwm Nantcol and she spoke in her interview with Richard Poole of the significance this particular Welsh landscape held for her: "Cwm Nantcol, in contrast, represents a retreat to a timeless, glacier-sculpted topography". When asked if it had changed her, she answered, "Not changed me. Confirmed, maybe, something I'd known and forgotten". Again, Stevenson shows her preoccupation with structure, as she does in the beautiful 'Red Rock Fault', dedicated to the memory of Frances Horovitz. Here, at the fault where limestone meets sandstone and life touches death, light falls on the landscape and describes it. In the same way the dead Frances Horovitz, glimpsed in her "boy's coat / on that sudden and slithery hill of stones" is seen in the same act of illumination and description: "You carried your love of that rushy place / in the candle of your living face / to set in the dark of your poems".

The dark of poems survives death; or may do so. There is a delicate balance between Stevenson's passion for the world as it is, a place where the most golden gorse that there will ever be is already flowering, and her impulse to make a poem. Only if the impulse that creates poetry becomes subservient to egotism does the balance fail. In 'Making Poetry' Stevenson urges that one of the poet's tasks is to "evade the ego-hill, the misery-well, / the siren hiss of *publish, success, publish, / success, success, success*". The tantalising susurration of this surely could not have been created by a poet who did not know the

nature of the Satan she was putting behind her. It could also only have been written by a poet whose sense of vocation is sharp.

This vocation, worked out over forty years with Stevenson's rare blend of disconcerting intelligence and sensory immediacy, is by no means yet fully defined. A poet of Anne Stevenson's calibre will continue to "inhabit, make, inherit" poetry. But while she writes, go out at once and buy her *Collected Poems*.

Helen Dunmore won the 1996 Orange Prize for her novel *A Spell of Winter* (Penguin).

Quodlibetical

JOHN BAYLEY SALUTES CHRISTOPHER REID'S NEW VOICE

CHRISTOPHER REID

Expanded Universes

Faber, £6.99
ISBN 0 571 17924 X

CAN IT BE THAT Philip Larkin has a true successor? One might have thought such a thing impossible, but Christopher Reid's new voice (well, not entirely new I'm glad to say, but a different kind of voice none the less) might well have caused the older poet – were he still with us – to cock a startled ear in Reid's direction. Could approval have followed? Knowing Larkin, from the Letters and from Andrew Motion's superbly unsparing biography, it seems most unlikely. But you never can tell. The old kelpie of the Humber could be swiftly and decisively generous when he read the real thing, and Christopher Reid's new book of poems is very much the real thing. The forty-four items in *Expanded Universes* are mostly but not all brief; and all are very good indeed. What about this for example.

Today my wife called me
    A "pompous old fart",
We were hugging at the time
    And did not spring apart,
though her words were deliberate
    and struck at my heart.

It's a fearsome business,
    this loving and being loved.
Would anyone try it
    if they hadn't been shoved
by a force beyond resistance,
    velvet-fisted and iron-gloved?

The ghost of Larkin is there, but the tone is different and of course the personality is quite different: the poem is purely original in its own way, let alone that Larkin always used an upper-case letter to begin a line. There is a certain piquancy in the fact, though, that if Larkin had ever been got to the altar his wife might well have soon been calling him a pompous old fart – he would practically have taught her to do so – and she would have done it with the same urge to stab affectionately. (Or, you never know, he might have ended up with a wife who would have used his own weapons of solitude and withdrawal.) Reid's rhyming is as brilliant as his, in being memorably emphatic while at the same time drawing no attention at all to the way it has been managed.

Indeed the poem, like most of its fellows, is memorable, in the sense in which Auden defined poetry as "memorable speech", and in a way which has become very rare indeed in contemporary verse. With the first line of any Reid poem one's attention is gripped immediately and held, line by exact line, to the end. This is a rarity which was already present in *Pea Soup*, Reid's second collection, but which was given rather too much of an emphasis by its

"Martian" connotations, There was a degree, not so much of arrestingness for its own sake, as of an amiable refusal to be too arresting, which could set up its own sort of predictability. 'Dear Diary', the poem quoted, has the absolute quality of Larkin's 'Forget What Did', and the same compression into the only possible public words of a personal and private reality. One cannot of course imagine Reid's self growing through words, like Larkin's, into the involuntary stature of an intimate legend. He does not seem likely to write his own equivalent of a 'Dockery and Son', but with so accomplished a poet, one never knows.

One feature of today's verse which is wholly absent in Reid is what might be called "post-modern diffidence", the tone often heard on Radio 3 readings in accents of pseudo-modest disclamation. Shall I ever be able to write this, the poet says, and to say what I mean? It's so hard, and one is just an ordinary person after all – all this delivered in lines, if they are lines, which would hardly qualify as prose.

In his most successful poems Reid's unstressed mesmeric accuracy produces a marvellous sense of what is happening at the moment the poem is being written, which eerily calls in question not only the assumed retrospection of poems but the apparent impossibility of "doing" them any other way. The poem's words have both the relaxation of the study and the terror of momentary actuality, fusing the two improbably together – in 'Scenes from Kafka's Marriage',

> A workman came to mend a cupboard door
> that would not shut. My wife had got his name
> out of the *Yellow Pages*.

The workman does the job in next to no time, but "When I took out my wallet to pay him / he still would not go; in fact he's here now". Our quotidian experience does indeed have such come-to-stay habits. It drinks endless mugs of tea

> and fills the bathroom with repellent smells.
> At night we can't sleep for the noise he makes,

obsessive and rodentlike, with bradawl and
> screwdriver.

'Distance' grips even harder. The words "peer down" from their desk

> into the walled yard
> where the tinies are left to play
> most of each weekday

and see rather terrible things apparently about to happen to "a bloblet in knitted gloves/gumboots and anorak". But there's no point in shouting. "With traffic between, and a shut window / it's too far from this desk".

"Tinies" and "bloblet" are, ironically, small chunks of verbal joy, mysteriously up-to-the-moment and state-of-the-art, like the complacent sound in the first line of another section of the Kafka sequence, "The theme of last night's dream was infidelity". Reid knows exactly how to use cliché, in such a way that it moves, amuses and dismays in equally hypnotic proportion. "The Thing and the Book", an obvious reference to the Salman Rushdie business, shows him able to move the reader quite simply and deftly to the point of nightmare. He is never rueful, nor lugubrious, but, like the great man from Hull who was both, he knows exactly how to give the reader the pleasure there is in dull and bad things, as well as in the things that are neither. *Expanded Universes* is a really rich little book: a joy to read, or rather to inhabit, for this poet possesses the secret of letting us, quite effortlessly as it seems, into his world. He and Mark Ford are the two poets who poems today I most look forward to; not that they resemble each other, but both have this same gift. Like Larkin, Reid is a poet who lives on in the mind, becomes part of one's own inner vocabulary. In every poetic generation there are not more than one or two like that.

John Bayley's new novel, *George's Lair*, has just been published by Duckworth. It completes, he says, "a trilogy of mild domestic thrillers".

A Sensible Reaction (on the whole)

by Atar Hadari

SOPHIE HANNAH

Hotels, like Houses

Carcanet, £6.95
ISBN 1 85754 252 5

SOPHIE HANNAH IS like Wendy Cope, they say, or "that's how they're trying to sell her" I am told, with the instruction that since I like the latter I should review the former. Hmm. Well, a reader of Ms. Hannah's second collection finds quite a different kettle of fish, and brightly coloured ones too, mostly.

It's not that she isn't as technically proficient as Wendy Cope, though at times she isn't. There are naff rhymes ("To last weekend and to the time I spent with you. / You left too soon and I was in a hurry so / I failed to mention maybe sharing rent with you. / Do I look sick? I eat a lot of curry though"), and the occasional metrical blip or mis-step (though I confess, having noted them on a first read-through, I can't actually find them now to point at.) The real difference, I think, is in the basic tone underneath the surface brightness.

These are predominantly love poems, of one sort or another, some disappointed, some enthusiastic. The overwhelming majority are pulled off with wit and panache, some are perfect anthology pieces which should be around for a good while:

Others will die instead of you
A fixed amount must die
(If there are quotas with these things)
And strangers' wives will cry
But I will have no need to say
I loved you and was proud
To be what I have been to you –
Your death is not allowed.

('Preventative Elegy')

The difference lies in the fact that where Cope's humour is underlain with grief, Hannah's project reveals itself as you go further into the book to be one of all but metaphysical, ethical exploration, and her metronomic heart is that of a scientist, weighing probabilities, possibilities. This book moves from an account of how certain lovers DID behave to how they SHOULD behave, to a questioning and analysis of possibilities of emotion. In this the ruling spirit is one of wit and common sense, and beneath the homey and day-to-day properties of her stage I think she is related to those seventeenth century courtiers whose loves were always transacted in a world of costs, odds, likelihoods.

When someone says they have a poet's soul
You can imagine laughing in their face
A sensible reaction on the whole
But he convinced me that it was the case
And that his poet's soul was out of place
What with his body selling advertising space.

('Selling his Soul')

There are occasional poems about craft, about the tunneller from prison camp who does not want to give up the tunnel merely because of liberation, and the occasional more opaque and open-ended moral piece like 'The Man Who Wouldn't Share His Garden with a Wolf', and if I saw a flaw to point to it would be that Hannah's talent seems at this point to be (as Kafka noted of himself on his death-bed) "still going in two directions at once" – there are the immensely polished and ready to lap up at one reading/hearing *tours de force* and then there are quieter, less certain, more exploratory and, perhaps, more thoughtful pieces – but the steady canter of the polished pieces makes one's ear less inclined to stop and re-adjust to the stranger music – it is as if John Lennon suddenly went from 'She Loves You' to 'Imagine' in one breath (and I don't know that Hannah is that good, I'm just making an analogy). I don't believe she'll have to choose between the two manners but, for me at least, the collection could have been arranged better to highlight the odder pieces, which are probably her escape route should delivering what's expected of her become oppressive.

The other criticism is that her language, while finely hewn, is transparent – I'm not sure if I'll recall a phrase that I could use to define some of my own emotions when next I am in one of the situations she describes (exception: "When his turned back makes one bed feel like two"). But her metaphors are apt and incisive, her patter funny, her intelligence unceasing and her experiments thoughtful – there's no knowing where she might go from here.

Caging the Minute

by John Greening

TESSA ROSE CHESTER

Provisions of Light

Oxford Poets, £6.99
ISBN 0 19 283262 X

LIKE OTHER WOMEN associated with our East Coast – Pauline Stainer, Anne Stevenson, Lotte Kramer – Tessa Rose Chester finds that fenland and crumbling cliff excite her to a spare, exposed clarity of word and image. The title poem, which ranges widely through 'Suffolk sky and sea', is one of those extended, on-the-hop, plein-air sequences that are close to this reviewer's heart. But there is a constant tension in this excellent first collection between that free-wheeling outdoor mood and something studiously interior. The point at which these two states might merge is what, I think, the poet is searching for (this is very much a quest book), and it explains why she opens with the words "My line returns from its walk ..." ('The Artist's Wife'). It is, after all, the fate of poets to be always walking away from the mental world of fine lexical distinctions into the broad-stroked wash of physical experience, then back again. Sometimes it is hard to decide which world is the abstract, which the tangible. 'Box' demonstrates well, with its neat syllabics, Chester's determination to make description revelation:

> A calm, still room. Prepared. Rows
> of polished gravers, spitsticks,
> scorping tools ready to make
> rounds and lozenges and squares ...

The poem painstakingly brings before our eyes the art of the engraver. But it is some of the shorter, less earnest, more abstract and musical poems that seem to successfully merge her technical skills with her sense of the mysterious. 'Twelfth Night' is a haunting lyric:

> A measure of snow
> in the difficult dark
>
> A measure of dark
> for the tree's distress
>
> A measure of distress
> at the turning year

> cut-glass birds
> on their last flight
> losing their sheen
>
> the finality of flame
> deepening the night
> the absence of green
>
> A measure of sorrow
> A measure of snow

That use of italics is characteristic (the need to objectify, to juxtapose, to set up tensions) and might be traced to Yeats, or set beside Eavan Boland's obsessive mythological waltzing with the natural world. Evidence enough here of Chester's technical prowess, her critical eye for words (consider 'distress'), her ear for internal sound effects. Elsewhere, she uses terza rima with refreshing ease, and brings off a triumphant double crown of sonnets (see 'The Minden Sonnets', *Poetry Review*, Spring 1996) – the best use of this extraordinarily tricky form since Neil Powell's 'A Cooling Universe'. In fact, her choice of so contrapuntal a verse pattern shows again her desire to make connections, and so find – as she puts it in a prose note to that Spring issue – "the bones of an answer". The way poems dove-tail in the collection is one of its most rewarding aspects. It ends, for example, as it began: with a short and somewhat abstract plein-air lyric ('The Naming of Parts') set beside a scholarly, dry-point "interior" about bees: 'Apologia: Apis mellifera'.

Tessa Rose Chester's poems are about ways of remembering and forgetting. She works as Curator of Children's Books at the Museum of Childhood, and – as she shows in 'Buttons', or 'Aspects of Amnesia' – knows that words are the most enduring repository we have, particularly in the face of: "This eating of the land, each relentless push, / / the constant rub and scour / that turns grand buildings / / into gravel . . ." It is perhaps because she is so conscious of the gradual decay of our church-prinked east that she is drawn to the safety of harbours, lighted pubs, country houses, rooms, boxes. In 'The Gallery' she even writes as if she were the room. Another poem begins: "A room of heavy beams, / ropes and planks; / a swelling ship / full of strangers. / / Change". Here, then, is a poet willing herself to capture in "a calm, still room" the seething minutiae of a passing life, while remaining alert to the huge abstract winds beyond. Churches collapse and drop into the sea. All a poet can do is recite their names. The rest is amnesia.

MONIZA ALVI
THE JOB

You have thrown the job to the stars,
but they return it despairingly.
They do not want it either.

You observe it jumping over the moon
more energetic than the cow.
It soars upwards – an ungainly creature

carrying on its back a freight
of appraisal documents and schedules.
It flies without you,

without your eyebrows,
your insight,
your frenzied anticipation,

your briefcase of improbabilities.
Wherever it lands
it will arrive on the dot,

or an hour or two earlier.
Open the post. Begin the day.

FLEUR ADCOCK
STOCKINGS

The first transvestite I ever went to bed with
was the last, as far as I know.
It was in the 60s, just before tights.
He asked if he could put my stockings on –
on me, I thought; on him, it turned out.
His legs weren't much of a shape,
and my suspender-belt was never the same
after he'd strained it round his middle.
But apart from that, things could have been worse.
The whisky helped.

I never went out with him again;
and I never, ever, told his secret –
who'd want to? (He must have counted on
the inhibiting power of embarrassment).
But I still went to his parties.
At one of them I met Yoko Ono.

ANNEMARIE AUSTIN
WATERSHED

I read about the centenarian woman potter
whose work – she said – continued as distraction
from too much thinking about young men.

It does not go away then – the sensual mental walk
up the inside curve of an arm, or the wish to press
the open mouth against a breast-bone thinly dressed
in skin, a longing to lie again in an embrace's cradle?

But what young man will think in an equivalent way
of the old woman bent above the potter's wheel,
or me, now at the watershed, seeing my once-smooth skin
begin its tiny pleating over and back from the bone?

I consider the future beyond the crest of this hill
with its downslope into solitude, where my flesh
will heal more slowly, where the ache of the phantom
of this amputation will keep me awake at night . . .

Though only alone was I ever graced by such as
that mole's sudden eruption a yard from my foot
when I sat and read in a drought-ridden garden –
and with such a live racket of tearing roots and
stems, such a commotion of insects in the grass.

PAULA MEEHAN
THE TANTRIC MASTER

For I shall consider his beautiful navel firstly
– an altar! – whereat I've often offered flowers,
the yellow buttercup especially, a monstrance I can elevate
to the memory of his mother who surely taught him to pet.
And honeysuckle and meadowsweet and the wild dog rose:
one for its scent, one for its sound, and one for the tone of his skin
that is all petal to me.
                For I shall consider
secondly each individuated pore of his entire body
and consider each at length having nothing better
to do with my time, and each being a universe unto itself.
This I call rapture.
                And thirdly, to make no bones
about it, being the crux, the hardest part of the matter,
I shall consider his noble and magical wand. He do good
business throughout the night with it. He enchant,
and spellbind and wind me round his little finger;
or, on a moony night in April, even his little toe.

Which brings me to his nails: he keepeth that trim and smooth
the better to pleasure me. So subtle his touch I can feel
the very whorls of his fingerprints and could reconstruct from memory
his mark on my breast. Each ridge the high mountain,
each trough the deep canyon, unfathomable;
but I, having buckets of time, do fathom, do fathom.

For I shall consider the mesmeric draw of his nipples,
like tribal erections on the broad plain of his chest,
megalithic power spots when I lay my hot cheek
on the cool of his belly and sight through the meadows
and the distant forests the trajectory of sun and other stars.

His mouth, I won't go into, being all cliché in the face of it,
except to say the dip of his lip is most suited to suction and friction,
and other words ending in tion, tion, tion, which come to think of it
when I'm in the grip of it, is exactly how I make sweet moan.
                For I shall consider
him whizzbang dynamo and hellbent on improving my spiritual status.

You can keep your third eyes and your orbs sanctimonious
the opening of which my Master believes *is* the point.
He says I'm a natural and ultimate enlightenment a mere question of time.
But in patient devotion I'll admit to deficiency. The theory of being –
not a patch on just being. Yap I distrust! Show me.
Don't tell me the way. The right place for talk of this ilk
is not during, not after, and foretalk will get you nowhere at all.
The best that I hope for in our daily instructions
is the lull between breaths, spent and near pacified.

JACKIE KAY
VIRUS

The mice come first. In our bedroom
at the top of the house we hear the cunning
scraping, scuttling inside the skirting.
It is the first sign.

The plague of flies are next. In our kitchen
at the bottom of the house, they swarm in sick
thick circles. It is late October.
The Pied Piper calls. "Something big", he says.
"Must be something big and rotten.

Look for the eggs, tiny, white".
This is the time of the Wests.
"Do you mean a body?" you say, anxious.
The Dalston train thunders by like fury

At the bottom of our town garden.
And yesterday the wasps came.
Two thousand strong. An army in my study
and the wee toilet. The Pied Piper returns.
"Vicious bastards", his eyes gleam with job satisfaction.

This is our love nest. I see you, looking at me.

ELIZABETH BARTLETT
GRAND MAL

The aura may be an intense feeling of despair
and sadness lasting for some hours, or on the air
the smell of carnations, before the eleven seconds
count down, and the shaking jerking fit,
the fall into nothingness. The spittle and urine
trickle away as the spasms get less, the teeth
release their hold from the tongue at last,
which feels bruised and swollen in the mouth.

Returning, he sits up and the faces gaze down.
He is ashamed to be so wet and dishevelled
and sleepy. There is an air of concern
and a turning away too. He disappears
and yet is all too evidently there to see,
frantic as an injured insect on the floor,
upsetting the onlookers. He is upset himself
and has no friends, for they are afraid.

Standing by the playground walls, the children
say "I nearly had a fit", then clap their hands
to their mouths. In his six years
he cannot understand why they do not smell
those violent carnations, or how they
have time to undo their zips, or keep their
tongues so sleek and fresh and pink,
and get asked to parties and to tea.

SMITA AGARWAL
MONSOON CANTATA

Rain is tattooing on the roof, tap-tapping
On the tin sunshade of the kitchen window,
Beating an insistent though erratic rhythm,
Deranged by dancing leaves that come in its
Way, like a chorus of mad women that seems to
Say – drench us, O drench us.

Across the barred, shut gate the road is
Gold and silver under the benign glare
Of sodium and fluorescent lamps; crimson
Tail-lights, tyres swish past. Criss-cross
Wires drip. A quiver of quicksilver water
Is rushing toward the gate – the barred, shut gate.

Something is knocking down that gate,
Something in connivance with the rain,
I turn my back to it, stare steadfastly
At the gas burner, at the metal frame of
Its round head with pricked-in holes.
Something has knocked down the gate,
Contralto voices come storming in,
Suicide-squad assassinations, communal
Conflagrations, scams, arms deals, a tribal
Woman gang-raped, mute deaths in custody,
India in the nineteen nineties. Something
Has knocked down a gate.

I turn on the gas,
Flare like the many
Blue, incandescent flames.

Away, the Lads

by Gillian Allnutt

The Forward Book of Poetry 1997

Forward Publishing, £6.95
ISBN 0 571 19000 6

EWART AND BRODSKY are dead. Even so, writes Alan Jenkins, "it hasn't been a bad year for poetry at all; it's been a perfectly good year". He should know: with fellow-judges Penelope Fitzgerald, Alastair Niven, Sean O'Brien and Michèle Roberts, he sifted through a record number of entries for the Forward Prizes.

Now in its fifth year, Forward gives prizes for the best poetry written in the English language and published in Britain and Ireland in the last year. The arrangement of the anthology reflects the categories: Shortlisted Poems from the Best Collection Prize; from the Best First Collection Prize; from the Individual Poems Prize; and Other Poems 1996. This year's anthology strikes me as a sane, solid, democratic selection. It's an unfussy one: no biographical details to be diligent about, just a list of acknowledgements to help you set out into contemporary poetry or into those parts of it you haven't yet managed to catch up with.

Though it is impossible to read John Fuller's poem 'The Garden' without remembering Eliot, there are few echoes in this anthology of the old exclusive Tradition. Now, with Robert Crawford, we can all be 'Chaps':

> The veldt is a chap, the heather's a chap,
> A great JCR of them tossing their caps
> Like schoolboys at Eton dyed red on the maps.

We're a jolly eclectic lot too. We are the inheritors – in the case of the English, undeserving, perhaps – of a language made richer by its colonial acquisitions. Now we can play, in Mario Petrucci's 'Top Our Road, Bottom Our Road', with the wonderful contradiction of 'Dis belief'. We can hear the thwack of the hurler's "sliothar" in Theo Dorgan's 'The Match Down The Park' – and perhaps only an Irishman could have turned the-most-boring-thing-in-the-world, sport, into one of my favourite poems in the book. We can persevere humbly with the footnotes to W. N.

Herbert's 'Featherhood' and know that the tenderness of this poem would be lost without its "pirrs an pirlies", its "prinklin", its "flaffin flicht". And we of the largest and least acknowledged colony of the old imperial dispensation, women, can rejoice with Eleanor Brown's exuberant poem 'The Lads':

> Your poetry belligerently asserts
> what nobody would trouble to deny:
> that you are the lads; that there you go;
> that yours will never be to reason why.

Mine it remains to reason why I find poems by Peter Porter and Allen Curnow, included here, quite impenetrable. I feel deficient (in masculinity), dim, intimidated. 'Away, the lads', then, gives me particular delight. I hope I am among the last generation of women to feel intimidated. Jenkins notes: "The Best First Collection list reverses the man-to-woman ratio of the Best Collections, as it did last year". He calls this reversal (this year's Best Collections: four men, one woman; Best First Collections: one man, three women) an accident. But I wonder. Now we know they fixed the eleven plus results; now we know girls do better than boys, particularly in language skills, all the way through school. Maybe this process of reluctant acknowledgement has still to come of age.

The protagonists in Andrew Waterman's 'Dora, Dick, Nip and Fluff' have done that with a vengeance:

> See Dick, flat out on a soiled mattress, clutch
> His head. He has the shakes. Dick drinks too much.

And Dora's on the game. And Nip's got stomach cancer. Which is too much. Without Dick and Dora – without the saving grace of books and being able to read them – I might not have survived the nasty, at the time unmentionable, realities of my own Fifties childhood.

I did survive – and long enough to read, and be immensely grateful for, Seamus Heaney's five-part meditation on Agamemnon, Clytemnestra, Aegisthus and Cassandra, 'Mycenae Lookout'. Maybe you've arrived at a definition of poetry when you can say – as Heaney says of those faced with the 'half-calculating bewilderment' of Cassandra –

> People
> could feel

a missed
trueness in them
focus,

a homecoming

This year's Forward anthology is an inclusive home. It's an inclusiveness that manages to resist the recent, pervasive, apparent need to "popularise" poetry. There's a lot of laughter in these pages, but the seriousness of the poetic undertaking is never sacrificed. No more is the responsibility for encouraging excellence: "Young poets", warns Alan Jenkins, "notation is not enough; cleverness is not enough". I take my hat off to that and to the judges. This is an anthology I shall not be ashamed to circulate among the least well read of creative writing classes.

Ogres and Angels

by Adam Thorpe

WANDA BARFORD

Sweet Wine and Bitter Herbs
Flambard, £6.95
ISBN 1 873226 17 9

ROSE AUSLÄNDER

Mother Tongue
translated by Jean Boase-Beier & Anthony Vivis
Arc Publications, £6.95
ISBN 0 946407 77 0

APART FROM GEOFFREY HILL'S mordant gleanings, and some memorable individual poems (Dannie Abse, David Hartnett), has British poetry addressed the Holocaust? Not really, surprisingly. Yes, mainland Britain was never occupied, and most British Jews escaped persecution, but many fled here, or settled after the war. My wife's relations were amongst these – her grandmother and aunt survived the war in Poland, keeping just one step ahead of the Gestapo. We drove to Poland last year with my father-in-law, to revive old memories and to seek out his grandfather's grave in the Jewish cemetery at Cracow. He died in 1936, and the names of the many members of the family who were murdered at Dachau and Auschwitz were chiselled on the stone ten years later. It was pouring, the cemetery was overgrown with brambles and nettles, and after two hours' fruitless searching in that lonely place, we gave up. My father-in-law showed overt emotion only once, in the Carpathian spa town where his uncle, a doctor, gave his services free to the poor for the summer months: a good and brilliant man, he injected himself, his wife, and his three children with cyanide when they were trapped at the Ukrainian border.

There are so many more such stories – and just from one family; yet how central are they to my father-in-law's adopted country? Not very, I would say. And that is perhaps the crucial difference between Britain and the rest of Europe. If poetry expresses a nation's soul, then Britain's soul is perturbed by things other than terror, betrayal, despair, guilt, the desire to forget, the need not to forget. But Wanda Barford's first collection, *Sweet Wine and Bitter Herbs*, is quite unapologetic about all this: her grandmother, aunt and uncle, and three cousins were murdered in Auschwitz, after a long passage in tanker and cattle-truck all the way from Rhodes, during which her grandfather was beaten to death by an SS guard. She herself fled Mussolini's Italy at the age of nine, was brought up in Rhodesia and settled as a young student in London, where she now lives with her family. In this sense, as she herself puts it, she writes "poetry in English, not English poetry".

The collection is subtitled 'Poems on being a Jew in the Twentieth Century' – and they are, above all, family poems: on her grandfather's boyhood in Izmir; visits to the Turkish baths in Rhodes with her grandmother; the rueful German-Jewish linen-merchant in Italy, selling them handkerchiefs monogrammed "with a J in the corner. But take care / it's not J for JUDE". We shift horribly easily into the fate of her twin cousins at Auschwitz, written as children's verse:

And mummy goes left
And daddy goes right
And Rachel, big sister,
Holds their hands tight.

They're told; twins are nice,
Should go to Hut 8
Let go sister's hand
And stand up straight.

Even the elegy for Primo Levi, 'The Shout',
builds the link between his suicide and his camp
experiences by concentrating on Levi's return from
Auschwitz – for two stanzas we are with his incred-
ulous mother at the top of the fatal stairs. In *Family
Snaps,* Barford tells us in an almost chatty manner
("Here's one of grandfather's garden in Rhodes")
about the sun-blessed childhood of "everyday
sorrows" and its dreadful end by interweaving the
two:

> Granny, survivors said, went into the gas-chamber
> carrying her soap and towel – she thought it was
> a kind of Turkish bath like the one she used to visit
>
> each Friday; I went with her
> and when we came back home
> it would be time to light the candles

These poems need little comment: they never
strain for effect or even attempt to explicate, but
work through the eloquence of poignant detail – by
this we shall remember them. The only angry
moments are as subdued as 'Practicalities', a Found
Poem which lists the companies (many still operat-
ing) whose names were "embossed on the side of
the oven" or printed on the crates full of Zyklon B,
and which Barford lets hang in the air as much as
the names on the suitcases found in Treblinka,
which end the poem. Like the sweet mulberries of
her grandparents' pre-war Greek garden, the very
modesty of Barford's verse highlights the unimag-
inable horror. In her ballad on the three hundred
Jews massacred in Vienna in 1181 (falsely blamed
for the drowning of three Christian boys), or the
later persecutions in Spain, she reminds us how the
Nazis, however psychotic, were not historical
freaks, but merely the most industrious and indus-
trial of Jew-killers.

Poetry seems the frailest of things to put up
against them, or their successors, but for Rose
Ausländer it was a principle of survival – another
"practicality" – in the ghetto of Chernotsy, in the
Carpathians. Like Danzig, Chernotsy was a place
of shifting ownership, situated on a political fault-
line, and the tremblings of calamity run right
through Ausländer's work. *Mother Tongue* gathers

the late flowering of this celebrated post-war
German poet, but it survives the passage into
English only faintly; its elliptic, rather severe
symbology needs to be fleshed by the "mother
tongue", I suspect. Unlike Barford, Ausländer
trades no stories with us: in the style of her wartime
friend Paul Celan, her sufferings are "sealed / in
hermetic silence" – as if the cellars in which she and
her mother crouched in hiding hold her still. A
litany of images – bread, dust, ashes, crystal, water,
moon and sun – seem, at first glance, too "poetic"
to enthral, and the effects have to be achieved
through the almost crystalline formation of the
unpunctuated lines, creeping down the page in
drop after drop of highly-compressed emotion.

Much of this emotion is bitter, even enven-
omed, coursing through those same images in a
disturbance of their usual associations and accreted,
pleasing familiarities. When she looks at the clouds,
she sees "ogres and angels" – in that order. When
she professes her faith "in the earth and its / danger-
ous mysteries", she sounds like a tiger prowling the
limits of its freedom: even the "mother" of language
can be "murderous". There is a telling silence and a
desperately important qualification after her defin-
ition of poetry:

> I profess my faith
>
> in poetry
> weaving humanity's myth
> in humanity

We know how dangerous myths are, and how terri-
ble a force "humanity" can be, and how salvaging
its second meaning here: yet Ausländer leaves us
troubled by it – what exactly is the expression on
the poem's face at that moment? Relaxed and smil-
ing, I doubt. Are we accustomed to this sort of
interpretative pressure from poetry in English? Not
really, with the possible exception of Beckett – and
he's much more forward with his despair, more
indulgent with his lacerations. But the last poems,
written in old age, contain some passionate hymns
to love, which is associated with "freedom / where
words / have all been lost". The German sound-
picture of Ausländer's poems – the tight-lipped
gruffness, the rolling beauty, the historical burden
(Goethe's tongue has been tainted for at least two
generations) – must provide much of what appears
to be lost here, but it is still an important glimpse
into a place where British poetry rarely treads.

Erning a Reputation

by Ian McMillan

MAURA DOOLEY

Kissing a Bone

Bloodaxe, £6.95

ISBN 1 85224 373 2

I HOPE I DON'T debase either of them by mentioning Maura Dooley and Eric Morecambe in the same sentence; Dooley isn't a comedian, of course, in the same way that Morecambe wasn't a poet. And yet, and yet … you know the way that Eric Morecambe could always place a word (or a pair of hands, like parentheses, round Ernie's wobbling chops) just so, to create the right effect at exactly the right time? It's the same with Maura Dooley: the words, the lines, the phrases are placed with great care and consummate skill, like feet on slippy stepping stones across a river in spate.

> … you know the way that Eric Morecambe could always place a word (or a pair of hands, like parentheses, round Ernie's wobbling chops) just so, to create the right effect at exactly the right time? It's the same with Maura Dooley.

Maura Dooley has lived much of her adult life surrounded by the sweat and endeavour of poem-making, as a centre director at Lumb Bank, as Literature Officer at the South Bank, as workshop leader, as editor; but it has to be said, with a note of triumph, that her work doesn't bear any of the hallmarks of Workshop Fatigue: Trembling Stanza Palsy or Careful Imagery Ague. Her work is fresh and vital, and that's a tribute to the stamina of her imagination and her craft.

Many poets struggle to make connections between the lumpy thing called Real Life and the shiny thing called Poetry. In poems that don't work you can see the join: the thick blue lines joining Life to Poem, obvious as the strings on Fireball XL5. With Dooley, you can't see the strings, you can't see the join, as in the tense, tight, novelistic, filmic opening of 'Heat': "Summer swells like a fruit. / Long evenings hang, the way small insects hug a storm lantern. / Already, we have forgotten about covers, / know that this will be called *that summer*".

What somehow begins to happen with poems like that, and with many of the others in the book, is that they assume, oxymoronically, a kind of surprising inevitability; after you've read the poem, you think "Yes, that's the way it had to be", like the first poem in the collection, 'History', with its central stanza about the disappointment of history-as-event: "Once I queued for hours to see the moon in a box / inside a museum, so wild it should have been kept / in a zoo at least but there it was, unremarkable, / a pile of dirt some god had shaken down".

The poems in the book range widely over loss, love and identity; there's a constant sense (perhaps a hangover from years of work as an enabler) of a need to make everything into a poem, which is the opposite of the Workshopper who wishes to make Significant Events or Epiphanies into poems with the addition of a few adjectives and a stanza about meaning. This approach means that subjects which could appear threadbare, such as ice on a pond, glitter with life: "Strangers exchange troubled smiles, / never dreaming before that the ice would have its own song, / a dull forgiving echo for those who stand at the side / / watching for cracks, those who don't know how to skate, / and those who try to read the hieroglyphs / under the soft muzz of scurf the dancers' heels kick up" ('Ice').

There are outstanding poems in the book, such as the prize-winning '1847', with its naked, weeping stanzas: "Ma's face is black with hair / her hands are paws. / She does not know me anymore. / Nights toss us cruelly. / Afraid I'll no more wake / I sit stony"; and 'Night Driving': "Turning a dial fills the air with static: / oceans, the blueness of night / and you own the road, the country. / The radio speaks only to you". But I think the book should be read as a whole, not as you might read a novel, or even a book of short stories, but as you might read through an atlas, as people sometimes do, captivated by the different routes, the range of landscapes, the lives encapsulated in shapes on the page. From Eric Morecambe to maps in a few hundred words: now that's a leap Maura Dooley would be proud of!

High Days & Holidays

by Linda France

JACKIE KAY, MERLE COLLINS,
GRACE NICHOLS

Penguin Modern Poets: 8

Penguin, £5.99
ISBN 0 14 058775 6

GRACE NICHOLS

sunris

Virago, £7.99
ISBN 1 86049 084 0

I HAVE TO say I came to reading *Penguin Modern Poets 8* already not liking it. I didn't like the cover – uninspiring and ill-designed. I didn't like the paper – rough and cheap, like a paperback novel. Didn't Auden say poetry was for high days and holidays? I didn't like the font used for the poem titles – too bold and its sans serif at odds with the main text. I think most readers are fussy about how a book feels in the hand, on the eye, as well as what's between the covers. Still I had high hopes of enjoying the poetry inside. That would make up for my aesthetic displeasure. I should have remembered that high expectations usually lead to disappointment.

Reading this book turned out to be rather like eating a sandwich where the bread is superior to the filling. Obviously you can't always have your book and eat it but if you are what you read, I'm happy to digest the qualities displayed in this selection of poems by Jackie Kay – playfulness, compassion, authenticity, honesty; and delighted by Grace Nichols – her strength, sensuousness, clarity, lightness. However I was less satisfied by Merle Collins' middle section – its ingenuousness, rhetoric, abstraction, and flatness.

To consider the least appealing first and so save the best till last – the pragmatic consumer's policy of delayed gratification: Collins' selection wasn't all bad but it certainly suffered from the juxtaposition, and inevitable comparison, with the excellent work of Kay and Nichols. And remember, I *wanted* to like what was inside this book – all the way through.

Collins' poems are literal in the extreme, failing

to present sufficient evidence of a transforming imagination at work to satisfy this reader at least. I became impatient with her abstractions, to use her own words, with her "Speaking so simply/of complicated things". For example:

As always, darkness follows the night
rainbow beauty, a spirit creation of fancy
and there I go willing beauty where none exists
watching molehills, willing mountains into shape
('Interlude')

This poem and many others are remarkable for their grammatical blandness, liberal use of cliché, repetition, subjective abstractions that convey little to the reader. And what exactly is "a spirit creation of fancy"?

It seems as if these poems were written more as therapy, as self-expression, in between the more demanding and important work of writing prose, than as crafted poems in their own right. Rather in the manner of May Sarton who said "I write novels to find out what I think and poems to find out what I feel". Surely a spurious distinction?

There are plenty of feelings here. Collins knows what moves her – "urgency . . . pain . . . power . . . strain . . . hope . . . doubt . . . sadness . . . force". But the trouble is they're not processed at all; as if the rhetoric alone was enough. The effect on the reader is not taken into account and so the effect is nothing much at all. I know that I find some of Collins' poems pleasing and well-crafted. Unfortunately they are not in this book.

Having said that, I do think that *Penguin Modern Poets 8* is worth it for the poems of Jackie Kay and Grace Nichols alone. It's just a pity the standard wasn't maintained throughout the book. This raised issues for me about how the selections are made. This one's definitely "Black Women", which seemed a touch demeaning. Some of the other volumes in the series are up to the same thing – "Scottish", "Women", "Humorous", "Working-class sympathies" etc. But then others aren't. Surely it's the poetry that counts rather than the poets?

Maybe it's a good thing that Penguin are risking unusual combinations, continuing the tradition of the original series. These volumes do serve as useful introductions to the work of new poets with whom readers might yet be unfamiliar. I like the way too that the poets make their own selections.

I already knew these poets' work and so I read the book in a different way – alert to selections, omissions, juxtapositions, moods. Jackie Kay's selection worked very successfully. It showed the range of her work from the emotional intensity of the very well-chosen extracts from *The Adoption Papers* sequence, through to the sulky blues of the Bessie Smith poems and the sad sensuousness of 'Dance of the Cherry Blossom' and 'Dressing Up'. Kay is particularly good at exposing injustice and cruelty: she pins down the pain of it in her direct approach, her measured tones and perfect, under-stated imagery, as in 'Hottentot Venus': "I hear their laughter like money shaking in a tin". She also skilfully evokes the innocence of childhood; underneath the laughter there's also sadness at its inevitable loss. This poetry goes in and stays there. Her voice is distinctive, sharp but generous.

Only one poem doesn't work for me – 'Dusting the Phone'. The extreme directness works against the subject matter somehow – the familiar situation of waiting for a new lover to call. The too-literal long lines fail to lift it somewhere else. The poem, like the phone, stays where it is and doesn't turn into something new, doesn't ring. Unlike 'Pounding Rain', which does:

We sat and stared till our eyes filled
like a glass of wine. I did it, the thing
I'd dreamt a million times. I undressed you
slowly, each item of clothing fell
with a sigh. I stroked your silk skin
until we were back in the Campsies, running
down the hills in the pounding rain,
screaming and laughing; soaked right through.

Grace Nichols' selection begins with an extract from *I is a long-memoried woman*, a graphic and moving sequence of monologues in the voice of a woman slave on a sugar plantation in the 'New World'. This sets the mood for all the rest of the section – poems about identity, oppression, migration, the domestic, "sex and death / ... always at the heart / of living". This is perhaps to suggest that these poems are just what one would expect but there are plenty of surprises. Nichols is an expert in subversion: "making a golden stool of the empire" of her oppressor's head; singing "the body reclining / As an indolent continent"; grease stealing "in like

a lover / over the body of my oven". She says: "Know that I smile / know that I bend / only the better / to rise and strike / again."

Her poems are the best sort of assertive – arising from a strong sense of self, not without a sense of humour. The pace is gentle and unhurried; the tone of voice, clear and strong, resonant with a certainty of conviction won from experience, an irrepressible positive attitude and a healthy imagination. The difference here from Collins is that we don't need to be *told* "They can kill our bodies, voices used to shout / in those days when the struggle was one struggle / they can never kill the spirit" ('To Trample Dreams': Collins). Nichols dramatises her resistance (as does Kay) and the poems are all the more powerful for that.

Grace Nichols

Her rhythms are song-like, child-like, while coming across as very, very wise. This whole section seems poised and truly graceful – dealing with important issues with a light and loving touch:

I have crossed an ocean
I have lost my tongue
from the root of the old one
a new one has sprung.

('Epilogue')

It was good to read this selection before *sunris*, Grace Nichols' new collection, to trace her discoveries, her changes. This book revels in a fascination for myth and legend, an excavation of spiritual roots. History is still an important theme but here it's as if Nichols has examined it and found it wanting: the power of the imagination goes deeper, lasts longer; and should be a part of history too.

The long title poem is a celebration of carnival: a conversation between the past and the present; a ritual assertion of independence; a procession of calypso songs; colourful and wayward, hypnotic and inspiring. The book rises towards 'sunris' beautifully and finally takes flight with 'Wings', a poem dedicated to the Jamaican poet, John Figueroa, "inspired by his comment that as Caribbean people we're preoccupied with Roots, when maybe we should be signifying ourselves by Wings".

Nichols' style is so unforced, it's deceptively casual but this is an elemental book, a force to be reckoned with, healing and nourishing.

Cassandra Calling

by Justin Quinn

ADRIENNE RICH

Dark Fields of the Republic: Poems 1991–1995

Norton,
hbk £18.95 ISBN 0 393 038 68 8
pbk £7.50 ISBN 0 393 313 98 0

THERE HAS NEVER been much point in criticising Adrienne Rich for letting politics spoil her poetry, nor in criticising her for being partisan instead of objective, angry instead of ironic. Because Rich, for many years now, has seen *belles lettres* – and especially the New-Critical type that glides "in mid-air, innocent" of the human mess below – as dead letters. The main achievement of her career has been to make the lyric form responsive to political change, more particularly, changes in the social status of women. In her best work (from the 1960s and early 1970s) the lines tremor with the anticipation of transformation, both of the body politic and of the bodies and minds of the people partaking of that change. Often the concluding revelatory lines of a poem seem to coincide with detonations of the social order, as in 'When We Dead Awaken' (1971) which ends with "a blue energy piercing / the massed atoms of a bedrock disbelief".

However, *Dark Fields of the Republic*, like so much of her work of the last twenty years (and there has been lots of it), is very boring. Poem after poem recyles the same oppositions and stock characters that have fettered her imagination for so long: we see the by-now hackneyed romanticisation of some heroic female figure facing "the age"; the familiar revelations of poverty and violence subtending suburban peace; the usual attempts to sympathise with "people under pressure"; and all this with a technique that hasn't budged an inch since 1973. No doubt this poetry is tonic for the troops, but even the troops must be getting tired of it by this stage.

Granted, Rich does occasionally question the validity of her identifications. In the poem 'Revolution in Permanence (1953, 1993)', she returns to the figure of Ethel Rosenberg, to whose memory she dedicated a poem in 1980, and repents somewhat:

What she is seeing I cannot see,
what I see has her shape.

. . .

I've worried about her
through the liquid window in that damp place.
I've thought she was coughing, like me,
but her profile stayed still watching
what held her in that position.

But these second thoughts, to me at least, just sound dutiful and pious; moreover, behind the solemnity of tone here is the quiet but firm presumption that what Adrienne Rich worries about and thinks about is intimately connected with the *Zeitgeist*.

Because, as well as all the recycling of themes and techniques, Rich harbours the ambition – voiced self-importantly in the book of essays, *What is Found There* (1993) – to be the Cassandra of the United States. This is unfortunate since Rich, thinking now purely in clichés and stock oppositions, is incapable of finding purchase on political reality. Robert von Hallberg, for instance, has fairly criticised her views of the marginalised as "patronizing and vulgar", revealing "no complications of the representations of identity one finds in the mass media". In both her prose and poetry, oppressed people – be they Jews in World War II Germany, coloured women poets in New York, exploited factory workers in California – are lumped together, the fact of their oppression erasing all individuating characteristics. This suggests that the mechanisms of Rich's imagination have more in common with oppressor than oppressed.

Her engagement with politics has finally served to dull her poetic capacities rather than enhance them. Nevertheless, Rich's own failure to achieve a convincing political vision in her poetry is no reason to doubt the validity of her insistence that "the question for a North American poet is how to bear witness to a reality from which the public – and maybe part of the poet – wants, or is persuaded it wants, to turn away". This seems valid outside North America also. However, the poets who will write this work will need intellectual and imaginative resources far surpassing those drawn upon in *Dark Fields of the Republic*.

Justin Quinn's first collection is *The 'O'o'a'a' Bird* (Carcanet, 1995).

JOHN WHITWORTH
STRUGNELL'S INCREDIBLE
LIGHTNESS OF BEING

I am a Modern Poet. People say
It's difficult to understand my stuff.
I tell them they're not up-to-date enough.
That's how it is with Poetry today.
I am a Modern Poet. And a bloke.
Most of us are. I think while Man creates
Woman inspires and appreciates.
Frankly, most Women's Poems are a joke:

Their sonnets scan. Their rondels rhyme. And worse.
Their volumes SELL! Of course they cannot hope
To pass as Poets in the Modern manner.
I scorn to live next door to Sophie Hannah.
No cocoa will I take with Wendy Cope.
Girls can't write Poetry.
                                   They write Light Verse.

Labours of Love

by James Keery

STANLEY COOK

Woods Beyond a Cornfield:
Collected Poems

ed. Peter Sansom
Smith/Doorstop Books, £9.95
ISBN 1 869961 47 1

FRANK REDPATH

How it turned out

ed. John Wakeman
The Rialto, £6.95
ISBN 0 9527444 0 6

STANLEY COOK'S ABIDING preoccupation is with memory – living and beyond death – and with its negations, neglect, anonymity and death itself. Numerous poems centre on memorials in the form of graves, statues, disused or demolished buildings; and many more are epitaphs for people the poet has known. Others reflect on the ephemerality of such phenomena as flowers, mills and "childish unhappiness". The wonder is not that Larkin's ghost should walk, but that it should be so effortlessly laid:

When the low full moon polished up by the cold
Lights up like the clock in a non-existent tower
I feel the daily pressure of work released
And a vacuum form that fills with embittered love.

Cook's "embittered love", trenchancy and "narrow-minded native praise" are comparable but rarely derivative, and his gift for the unchallengeable image is a shared rather than an inherited one. Cook published only in magazines until the seventies, but the two poets, born in the same year, both came to maturity in the forties; like Larkin, Cook is able to combine the intelligent scepticism of the Movement with the profundity of Apocalyptic modernism, for example in 'Second Eleven at De La Salle College', an early poem in which "A priest comes down from the school to watch the match":

Was it right when part of me told him
To live his kind of life? The genitals of prayer
Seem small to sow the void and love seems easier
When whether I will or no my body makes me care.

The alternatives of love and celibate self-dedication are the theme of Larkin's earliest great poem, 'Waiting for breakfast, while she brushed her hair' (1947), yet the astonishing "genitals of prayer" recall Dylan Thomas at his best. In a very different vein, 'Ebenezer Elliott, the Corn Law Rhymer' averts its gaze from Elliott's statue ("It was not this dogs' convenience wrote the poems") to pay tribute of its own through gritted teeth:

Now we eat untaxed our flannel slices
Of steam-baked bread: but anger remains
And days that like our souls are fiercely dark.

An "intensely private man", according to his editor, Peter Sansom, who rightly draws attention to his "courage" and "ambition", Cook is in no limiting sense a modest poet; nor had he any reason to be so. In an eve-of-fiftieth-birthday lyric, '11.4.72', he firmly denies that he had "ever wished to obtrude myself", but against this principled abstention must be set his heartfelt commiseration with John Clare – "time is maddening enough . . . without the world's neglect" – and 'On my Birthday: 11 x 4', whose characteristic images "I like to think that none but me could reveal". It's true that MacCaig springs to mind once or twice – "A slate falls from their roof but turns into / A pigeon and puts itself back in place"; Andrew Young, perhaps – "The hard catkins, as yet unexpanded, / Queue for Spring along the branches of the silver birch"; even, anachronistically, John Ash – "Pity everyone / Who had, like him, to swim for it in the Thirties, / Fully clothed in the nation's economy"; but the more I read Cook, the less he sounds like any other poet.

I remain unconvinced by the 600-line title poem, regarded by Douglas Dunn and others as a "masterpiece". The narration of a young girl's murder is uncharacteristically cynical and the apostrophes on the theme of corn remain disjointed jottings. There are some deft digs at the murderer, who "makes himself at home in prison, / Hurt that no-one who knew him pays him a visit"; but the real villain of the piece is Tennyson, "Immortalising literary / As well as social inequality . . . animating rustics to amuse their betters". Unfortunately, on this showing, 'Maud' knocks Cook into a cocked hat. The poem is redeemed by its evocations of local people, including a sometime "slender, blue-eyed and golden-haired . . . village beauty" with a hardy resistance to symbolic corn:

She lives in the selfsame yard with her children,
The blue of her eyes diluted, a tall thin woman
Raising her washing to let them deliver the coal.

Leaving teaching, Cook resigns himself "to being remembered / By someone and for something I forgot"; leaving Huddersfield, to being "one / of the many who anonymously / Fill the blanks in its history". 'Day of the Second Funeral' asks two startling questions: "Who wishes to be insured against mortality / And what has anyone that deserves to be preserved?" In answer to the first: if not everyone, at least every poet. Part of the answer to the second is this beautiful book, a labour of love on the part of its publisher. For its images, certainly – singles on a carpet "Like overlapping lilies on a pond"; office-blocks in the rain that "Dissolve like cubes of jelly in a bowl"; for gallows humour – "Aptly the chapel of rest is down a one-way street"; for compassionate dogmatism – "Even for Paris – / or Helen – you oughtn't to do this to your son" – *Woods Beyond a Cornfield* "deserves to be preserved"; but most of all for those evocations of people – the ex-colleagues portrayed in 'Staff Photograph': 'Grandfather Jacques', "Always correct, even to sending one son / Away from Sunday dinner for putting vinegar / on hot meat"; 'Mr Wheeler' – "anything measured and sawed / He fits so snugly he seems to be putting it back"; 'Betty', "with too many children, / Tewing her inside out to feed and dress them"; and 'Tom', who shared the poet's "forgotten boredom" of a childhood, and who elicits his most intimate lines:

If I earn more, it might have been otherwise;
And if I am happier, I apologise.

Frank Redpath

is another poet whose "patchy publishing history has almost prevented him having the chance to be underrated", as Sean O'Brien puts it in his introduction (the more credit to John Wakeman for his own labour of love). Like Cook, Redpath "was a good deal more interested in writing poems than in publicising his existence". I was surprised to find O'Brien so defensive about the "supposed influence" of Larkin, for I'd wonder about any critic who failed to discern it. The poems acknowledge their indebtedness with good grace, their technical range confined within Larkin's but also a reminder of its breadth: from iambic stanzas seeded with polysyllabic negatives, such as 'Lunar' (surely a good-humoured glance at 'Solar'?) –

Improbable as ever stands
The moon in mid-day blue, blue-shadowed, thinly
                                                    gleaming,
Washed to a rag. How disturbing, still, that
Inappropriate presence, that unrelenting,
Wrong-time stare. It shouldn't watch us waking,
Busy with lawful business, rational demands –

– to the metrically unpredictable surrealism of 'From Our Cycling Correspondent' (cf. 'If, My Darling'). And Redpath's finest poems are undiminished, not least because of the temperamental differences discussed by O'Brien and illustrated by the marvellous 'Miss White'. The poem begins with the speaker "Fumbling along the landing to the loo", but sends the vulgar ghost of Larkin "groping back to bed":

What I'll miss now is that surprising ghost
Who'd march in there to join me, climb into
My dropped pyjama trousers, make a nest.

Absurd familiar I named Miss White,
Gone, now, taking your gift, laughter at night.

O'Brien makes an illuminating comparison between 'A Lyric' and MacNeice's 'Meeting-Point', but Redpath surpasses MacNeice with a brilliant reversal of 'Sad Steps', managing an *ascent* from high-flown musings to an impolite epiphany:

Something is happening that never, ever,
Happened to anyone before, he thought . . .
Taking each eye in turn, she painted it
Using a brush, a block of black, and spit.

My own favourite is 'A Walk in the Evening', in which the poet is tempted away from "firelight . . . and the smell of cooking" by a view of rain six fields away, "over that ragged / Edge of the rising land":

To set out for the rain would be perverse . . .

Only, that stubborn fidget to be moving
Hangs over us from childhood, when we could
Believe that falling band of grey was not
Rain, but a more than natural event –
Like water rising up to meet the sky –
And, more, that when we reached it we would be
In it, yet see it as it looked from where
We saw it first. We know better now.

But all the same it's tempting. Who's for a walk?

PENELOPE SHUTTLE
HOUSES

Also
I know of houses in the suburbs

where people deep-freeze their tears
in yoghurt tubs

and fax
their smiles worldwide,

plank-walkers singing as they dive
down greenfrog depths

of sleep's pond,
seeking the lace

of a leisure still being woven there
in an allurement

of artless sifting waterlight
"without sacrificing perspicuity to ornament": *

oh but
"that the world is whole

every day
and always chained": **

those terrible cries
from the boys' prison at Ashford,

the smells from it denying
the deep lovely indiscreet smells of infancy;

(trimming the bassinet
and asking for so little:)

child, your sorrows are my sorrows,
your joys my joys,

yes, even in the Maison de Dédalus,
winding shadowe-house,

echoes from the painted walls,
stories made from someone's blood:

oh but also

there is the cliff path
where the newly-hatched rabbits

baby through the showers
and dusk bows to us

with Chinese promises,
"blue in a cloud-swept sky", ***

a waterlogged raft of lilies,
a pagoda on a shore:

house which is neither prison,
orphanage or torture tower,

is painted rose and scarlet,
gold and sun,

and look,
has no door in, not one.

* Alexander Pope, *Essay on Man.*
** Hölderlin, trans. David Constantine.
*** P'u-Su Mu Che, trans. Duncan Mackintosh and Alan Ayling in *A Collection of Chinese Lyrics.*

MEDBH McGUCKIAN

BUTCHER'S TABLE

We flew between two sheets of heavenly blue
which crossed the top of the world.
Bank notes fluttered on pavements, and in cool,
arched rooms, eyes matched conversations.

He played me a little sad Chopin, the blue-
out was bright, but the fields were a strange
sour green. At some indefinable signal
a hundred horses moved as one, storks in migration

landed on power cables and burned in blue flames.
Some of the tallest are the shortest now,
the burn cases lie so still, beyond forgiveness,
dark marks show how deep the water rose.

Once again we are alone in the war,
we have torn the skin off rooms like dolls' houses,
we have sown the cemetery with mines, a jigsaw
of bodies mulls the dust. If Overlord has started

you must make the gun part of your arm, squeeze it
like an orange in your palm, write with it as a prayer-
like pencil. But what a little life the dead tanks can take,
as they repair our country, with my gun arm against the door.

SUSAN WICKS
EYE DOCTOR

This is the blindness of snow,
escape of the blood, dead dream
of a world that is wrapped, given.

No body under this sheet, no flesh
rising and falling, the white eyelids
smooth as a child's, unwrinkled.

By the path, a blur of tree-trunks
without shadow; my plodding boots
sink into cloud, a matt whiteness.

The road stretches ahead of me,
its lace of yellow tyre-tracks
reimagined as the sky

pours out its cold hiss. So many
white moths touching
my cheek, dancing and receding

as if into dusk. I close my eyes
and see red, the bright cells
of my retina, the pulsing hive

crawling with life. Oh, but at 2 a.m.
through the huge uncurtained windows
of my cabin, the gentle dark.

CAROLE SATYAMURTI
THE LIFE AND LIFE OF HENRIETTA LACKS

That was me in the New Look
sassy as hell, in the days
when wicked was wicked;
not the fist on hip of a woman
who knows she's cooking
a time bomb tumour;

not a number's up smile
like a dame who figures
she'll not be getting the wear
from all those yards
of cloth she's scrimped for,
who'll be dead at thirty.

Dead? For forty years
my cloned cervical cells
have had a ball in Petri dishes
gorging placenta soup,
multiplying like their crazy mother
– the first ever cell line,

flung like spider's thread
across continents I never got to visit,
the stuff of visions, profits,
reputations in Melbourne, Baltimore;
hot property, burning mindless
energy I'd have known how to use.

They never asked. Never said
how's about you live for ever,
like immortal yogurt? I'm bought,
sold like cooking salt. But I get even,
grow where I'm not supposed,
screw up experiments.

Soon, they'll have the know-how
to rebuild me from a single cell.
A rope of doubles could jitterbug
from here to Jupiter. Meantime,
I practise my piece of the action,
hungry to cry my first cry again.

Henrietta Lacks died in 1951, but her cells live on in test tubes around the world.

CONNIE BENSLEY
ENGLISH DICTATION

I

I woke up from my nap. The clock struck four.
I thought I'd go out on a City Tour.
I rang Reception. *Tours leave on the hour.*
I booked one: but the rain began to pour.

Still, better go. It made me think of our
débâcle when we spent the day in Tours.
The trees were caked with ice and white as flour.
We got lost in the snow and found that dour

café – where waiters (and the wine) were sour.
The former looked askance at our amour.
Quite right. It ended. Now I just devour
my guide books on another lonely tour.

II

The tour raised up my spirits from their trough.
We drank some wine. I met a man from Slough
who got us singing on the coach – although
I got fed up with 'Blossom on the Bough'.

But when I staggered back I felt quite rough.
I rang Reception, said: *I've got a cough.*
I need some pills and whiskey. She said: *Tough.*
I saw you coming in. You've had enough.

ELIZABETH GARRETT
TRIPTYCH

I

First frost. The cumulus of breath
We stoop through to collect the tart harvest;
Each day a different constellation, less
Random than the last. See how the grass
Retains the acid green and aftermath
Of weight, the precise gist of appleness.
Just so. The day your chilled fist
No longer fits in mine to take its warmth,
The apples and the frost will go unnoticed.

II

In this wide garden chance has planted
A child; hunkered in earth, neat as a bulb,
The nib of his head points heavenward.
He is all gathered in time, at the hub
Of the seasons' wheel, the only hour he knows –
The immutable noon of love when the big hand
And the little hand conjoin. Dusk loosens
Its damp knot. It is time to move on.
The heart quickens, then slows, to the thin
Bright beat of the bell at Evensong.

III

Daddy's boy. Not so. You are your own
Despite appearances; feet on the ground,
Running. In our belfry we wait for the wind
To come, speaking in broken whispers of
Ourselves, the rich dissonance of love.
When words fail, our breaths rise and fall
Across your name's hushed vocable.
What recalls us to ourselves is not the founding,
Nor the fundamental, but the low thrill
Of the hum note outliving the swung bell.

PAULINE STAINER
THE FLIGHT OF ICARUS

"What happens to the molecules is one thing: what happens in the onlooker is less calculable by far" – Francis Spufford

How long did it last?
And is it still going on
for those who look up
from the lawn
with the kings and angels?

He is the sun's whipping-boy
flying into
the unseizable sign
which says
Deepen me.

Paint him
with raised brush-strokes
impasto –
all the big cats
kill with a neckbite.

And this particular body
this wax
that gives out a sound
if you tap it
with your knuckles

Look up –
unio mystica
where he catches the light
like a gilt shroud-pin
under the vapour trails

the gold hawk
with glass inlay,
etched on the zenith
like a clove
of Paradise.

As he suckles
he hears

the maternal heartbeat
in the background,
engine and ichor

the *duende*
of great sunlight
smoking the wax
until it runs
like anointing oil.

Which goldsmith
cast the sun
in a single piece
when he is fletched
with so many tongues

dropping seven skins
like a salamander,
as if he could
reassemble himself
before sundown?

in such a multitudinous falling
we expect sound
a winch to lower the angels,
the hiss of saltpetre
from undersea scars

the sky repeated
exactly in the water,
the sun's hawser
burning his hands
to the bone.

It fools the eye –
the discerning gesture –
the error on red
that makes an art
of bearing pain.

O Preposterous Vocative!

by Maggie O'Farrell

PENELOPE SHUTTLE

Building a City for Jamie

Oxford Poets, £7.99
ISBN 0 19 282517 8

PAULINE STAINER

The Wound-dresser's Dream

Bloodaxe, £6.95
ISBN 1 85224 370 4

I'LL ADMIT IT straight away: I'm probably not the best person to review Penelope Shuttle or Pauline Stainer. I have a strong and irrational aversion to two things in life: one is people who insist on relating their dreams to me in excruciating and unencouraged detail. The second is poets living after about 1930 who start sentences or lines with the exclamation "O" ... The latter never fails to bring to mind the irritating speech patterns of the housekeeper in *Doctor Findlay's Casebook*. Both these poets, at some point in their new collections, do one or the other. In particularly irksome poems, they do both.

Building a City For Jamie makes me wonder if Penelope Shuttle suffers from narcolepsy, so much does her poetry revolve around dreams. I have nothing against dreams or dreaming: I just happen to believe that they are an ancilliary and often entertaining extra to life. Shuttle, however, appears to believe that dreams and their surrealism define life more faithfully than conscious experience. Much as Jeanette Winterson claims that "Our real lives are elsewhere: art finds them", Shuttle would probably maintain that dreams are our real existence.

In 'January 20th, 1993', she asks "What does it mean ... to wake up coming? / ... in a bed that isn't the bed I'm sleeping in / but still belongs to the dream / and all its absolutes". She keeps us waiting for the answer until the final stanza, which is staggering in its glib crassness:

> It's as if every orgasm is the first, I guess,
> and laid end to end the whole lot brings hours
> of happiness – especially valuable
> in a world ravaged by war and tourism.

I'm sorry – you just can't say things like that and get away with it. 'Eight Frog Dreams' isn't much better; with a title like that how could it be? It is not often that poetry make me ask, "So what?" but it's the only response I can muster when faced with stanzas like these:

> But the frog cries thus – Grook, Grook, Grook.
> Or – Quar Quar Quar. (Its nuptial pads shining.)
> Or – Oop Oop Oop.
> Or – Keck Keck Keck.
> Or – Bree ke-ke-ke. (This last one is purred.)
>
> A frog in a dream
> is worth two in the hand.
> Do not be my enemy, says the dream-frog.

Her poetry relies less on metaphor than on visualization or anthropormorphisation: in her descriptions, the attributes or properties of things take on a physical significance. It is the "thingyness" of things that concerns her. The description of a tomato is a mixture of tenuous definitions and sense-impressions: "It is rude, straddler of categories, / a renegade, a pseudo-apple. / Wolf-peach, were-peach ... The tight skin pops, splits, yum, / seeds spatter against the deep-probing tongue". She likes definitions but her tendency to overdefine produces the opposite of the desired effect, leaving the reader floundering in a confusion of too many insubstantiated statements:

> Frogs prefer lengthy monologues,
> not cabaret songs.
> They do not paint their faces.
> In a fairy tale a frog can do magic things ...

Her poetry can be frustrating and tiring, and is like nothing so much as watching someone you don't know very well play word-association games by themselves. Most frustrating of all is her fondness for raising questions she does not bother to answer, the most extreme example being found in 'Some Rivers':

> Who paints hands on my door? Who has some
> rivers? Some things?

Some hands painting some hands on some doors?
Who has some stars? Some rain? Some clouds at
                                    night? Some biscuits?

I'm not surprised she didn't get round to tackling
those – I couldn't be bothered either. Her poetry
works best when anchored in specifics, or when the
surreal feyness of her style is undercut by a certain
savageness. The woman in 'Postman' is tormented
by an enigmatic postman who reads her letters aloud
and then offers annoying and singularly unhelpful
advice like, "yes, study the poets". As he leaves, she
is "already ringing the kennels, / ordering a big
young devoted-to-me dog: / tomorrow he will stand
guard by my gate". In 'Sweet Heart' the woman
woos her lover with a kind of empowered supplica-
tion – "It is for you ... I carry the sky on my back. /
It is for you I eat so many large meals, to become
strong" – and then points out to the voiceless man a
sea with "deep tarnish-green waters" in which there
is the "angel-swoop / of passing shark ... he glides
away in narrow-minded self-absorption". It is an
astutely discomforting end to the poem – I just wish
there were more sharks, and fewer dreams.

Pauline Stainer

as chance would have it, offers an insight into
Shuttle's dream obsession. 'The Sleep Laboratory'
depicts a Brave New World scene where the sleep-
ers' "rapid eye movements [are] monitored ...
temples wired". It could be interpreted that poets
are the "precision instruments for dreaming",
recording every flicker, every minute alteration in
the mind during sleep. She conveys only contempt
and horror for the waking world which is a "glimpse
of livid hellebore" – paradoxically, an artificially
drugged state; justice for Persephone, "for the
flower she plucked". At times, Stainer's work crack-
les with an intensity of feeling. Much of it centres
around the edge of experience: "edge" in the sense
of knife-edge, the very acutest point. 'Ruskin takes
Rose La Touche to the Crystal Palace' shows him in
a needle-sharp agony of sense that paralyses him,
rendering him incapable of action:

> They do not touch ...
> But he trembles
> at her slight body
> solarised against
> the glazing-bars,
> the sun behind
> the quinine tree

swinging
her polished axe.

Just having "her letter in his breast pocket" is enough
to bring him to a moment of epiphany that makes
"him kneel / suddenly on Skiddaw / and invoke the
Litany". She draws on a rich variety of sources –
myths, literature, science, the Bible. Darwin, in
'Darwin in Patagonia' is depressed and assailed by
difficulty and doubt, brooding "on the process / of
perfection and the less perfectly gliding squirrels ...
never completely well". Even though he is absorbed
in recording "the diving thrusts ... the ice floes /
which may formerly / have transported foxes", he
still dreams "of Adam naming / the doubtful species
/ and wake[s] shuddering / at the irreproachable
design / of the eye". Stainer's universe is that of a
balanced symbiosis: there can be no faith without
doubt, no love without agony, no violence without
a kind of tormenting justice – Gilgamesh, after
mindlessly slaughtering lions, is unable to slough off
the experience because: "Years later / they rose up
before him / in the underworld ... he felt again / the
strange rubato / of his own heart / beating with
theirs / several minutes / after extraction".

She invokes brilliantly that moment where the
sacred and profane can intersect and fuse. 'A
Christening By Snowlight' interweaves religion,
geography and the physical body: "In a bridge-
shaped chapel ... lilt of the river / flowing blackly
below. / We stand in a light trance". When the water
hits the child's head, the mother feels "the milk
welling / like a hot tincture / inside her blouse".

'Chromatics' is a poem of obscure power, the
story of a blind girl, "a touch player ... at the glass
harmonica". She seems to personify Stainer's world
where everything is enmeshed and connected. When
she is "running wet fingers / round the rim / of each
revolving bowl", she is able to feel "the altered
element – fiery circles / the susceptibility of things /
to hold colours / not their own". The final stanza
conveys the drunkeness of things being unified:

> But how does the ear
> conjure the eye
> when, playing to an audience
> I hear the glass-blower's breath
> flood each of their heart-chambers
> in turn?

I can probably forgive her for the odd "O we flowed
once ..." or "O wave and particle ...".

Not Crude but Clever

by Sophie Hannah

GAVIN EWART

Selected Poems 1933–1993

Hutchinson, £9.99
ISBN 0 09 179176 6

THE POEM 'Office Friendships' ends with the lines:

Sex suppressed will go berserk
But it keeps us all alive.
It's a wonderful change from wives and work
And it ends at half past five.

The rhythm is jaunty and the poem appears light and effortless, but anyone who works in an office will instantly know what Ewart is talking about and will realise, if they were not aware of it already, that daily life without sexual intrigue would be so dull as to make it hardly worth bothering getting out of bed in the morning. However, it is essential that this intrigue should remain suppressed and end at half past five, posing no real threat to family or career. This is just one example of how Ewart's talent works: he can sound jolly and frivolous, but at the same time, in the space of four lines, he can sum up the motivating forces behind most people's lives.

Another poem, 'Short Time', accurately describes the way that people deceive themselves in order to make their dreams seem real: "Bad breath, the thickening corpulence, / The faded, bloodshot eye. / / This is his dream: that he is still attractive". The poem first tricks the reader into feeling contempt or pity for this deluded "florid business-man of fifty", and then ends with the line: "Such dreams are common. Readers have them too".

There are moral lessons to be found in Ewart's poems, but he never hectors the reader, nor is he a killjoy. In the poem 'Hurried Love', he points out that it is not necessarily sordid to go for a quickie: "She may have a train to catch; perhaps the / room is theirs for one hour only . . .". This poem makes a serious point: romance and pragmatism can co-exist. Booking a hotel room for one hour only isn't seedy – it's sensible. Or, as Ewart says: "Not crude, but clever / are those who grab what soon is gone forever". Having read those lines once, I couldn't forget them if I tried. They are firmly lodged in my mind and ready to be whipped out, should any allegations of sordidness ever be hurled in my direction.

Ewart's poems are meaningful because they say so much about people. He is wise, compassionate, funny and honest. He handles emotional subject matter with great skill, neither neglecting the emotion involved nor weeping all over the reader, as in the sonnet 'The Last Things': "Then there are last words, variously reported . . . / My father said (not last perhaps): Say goodbye to Gavin". Sadly, we have all had to say goodbye to Gavin, but it would be extremely unwise for readers to say good-bye to his poems. There's a poem in this collection entitled 'It's Hard to Dislike Ewart', which is true, although I didn't try. In the poem 'Poets', however, he makes plain his opinion of people who do:

We all want total praise
for every word we write,
not for a single phrase;
we're ready to turn and bite
the thick malicious reviewers,
our hated and feared pursuers.

Many poets have written responses to critics and/or criticism, but not many have poked fun at themselves at the same time. This poem ends with the lines: "we wander free, or rhyme, / our admirers not very many – / lucky, perhaps, to have any".

Ewart's reputation owes nothing to luck. He deserves it. In the poem 'The Gentle Sex' (1974), he abandons his usual happy tone in favour of a more harsh one as he describes the murder of a woman in horrifying detail:

Oedema of the brain,
associated fractures of the skull,
and on the scalp the deepened main
sixteen separate wounds. Dull
their lives must have been, dull and dull indeed
for this to be their pleasure! The wayward gull
floats over Belfast; animals have no need
for torture. Her face was completely black. And
certainly, chewing gum in court, they'd do it again.

This is one of the longest poems in the book and the formal skills that went into it are quite incredible. Ewart's disapproval and disgust here are particularly powerful when contrasted with his loveable-old-softie tone in some of the other poems.

All in all, an excellent selection from the life's work of a wise, witty and versatile poet. I hope this is the sort of "total praise" he wanted.

Otherworldly yet Clay-footed

Jane Dowson

RUTH PITTER

Collected Poems

Enitharmon, £10.95
ISBN 1 870612 140

THE REVISED *Collected Poems* has been timed for 1997, the centenary of Ruth Pitter's birth. The 1990 edition – which cheered her final years before her death in 1992 – is now out of print, as are her 16 volumes of poetry. From 1920, she had a healthy publishing history for seven decades, gathering tributes and literary awards all along the way; most notably, she was the first woman to be awarded the Queen's Medal for Poetry in 1955.

Pitter's preface to *Poems 1926-66* (1968) is partly responsible for the oxymoronic image of the poet as a light-hearted visionary: she aimed to show the human capacity for experiencing both "agony and enormous bliss". One benchmark of her poetry is undoubtedly a sensitivity to suffering, allied to an almost absurdist detachment. The tributes by admirers, who include John Betjeman, Roy Fuller, Thom Gunn, Robin Skelton and Kathleen Raine, in *Ruth Pitter: Homage to a Poet* (1969) depict an otherworldly yet clay-footed poet who sought to articulate the shafts of sunlight glimpsed in the garden. When held in its entirety, however, it is difficult to signpost this wide-ranging and complex *oeuvre*.

The poems can be read for signs, although not necessarily as a chronicle, of the key events and phases of Pitter's life: childhood in the East End of London, employment with the Walberswick Peasant Pottery Company in Suffolk and her crafts and furniture business in Chelsea account for her ease with a variety of speech registers and a common touch which never patronises the underdog. Her long-standing connection with A. O. Orage and his socialist journal *New Age* indicates her democratic principles; she rejected high modernism, believing Eliot to have contributed to a "disaster" in English poetry, by "taking it away from the common man and making it the property of the few". She started at the University of London but left when war broke

out. Her war work in both world wars is behind some of her best poems: 'To a Lady, in a Wartime Queue' and 'Victory Bonfire' were selected for the sadly out of print anthology of women's second world war poetry, *Chaos of the Night* (Virago, 1984). The *Collected Poems* are worth buying just for these and other, often retrospective, meditations on war, like 'Funeral Wreaths':

In the black bitter drizzle, in rain and dirt,
The wreaths are stacked in the factory entrance-yard.
People gather about them. Nobody's hurt
At the rank allusion to death. Down on the hard
Cobblestones go the painted girls on their knees
To read what the football-club has put on the card.

Pitter's gradual conversion to Christianity during the second world war may have translated into visions, such as 'The Great and Terrible Dream' – a confrontation with the bloodied crucified Christ – but there are dramatised encounters between the living and the dead all through the collection. The deep-down convictions work best when concentrated on the psychological states of faith and doubt; 'Lame Arm' (from *End of Drought*, 1975) for example, explores the problem of pain through the protests of different wounded creatures. There is no ethereal piety here. In 1952, with her business partner Kathleen O'Hara, Ruth Pitter moved to Buckinghamshire where she became respected for her knowledge of plants and vegetables. These, along with birds, flowers and trees, crop up throughout her poems but always with an allegorical purpose. 'Stormcock in Elder' tells of economic imbalance through a hermit's visitation from an angel: "one half of the world, or so they say, / Knows not how half the world may live; / So sing your song and go your way". In old age, ill-health and increasing blindness did not snuff out her social concern, self-sufficiency and sense of humour.

The chronologically arranged *Collected Poems* invite the how-did-she-develop line of enquiry. It is possible to detect a plainer idiom and generally shorter lines in the later poems, yet the characteristic structural irony is as evident in the mock-heroic first poem 'Maternal Love Triumphant or Song of the Virtuous Female Spider', which satirises idealised motherhood, as in the parodic couplets of the late 'Pot-Bound', where the voice of the stunted plant begs for 'Food and Space'. Such play with form and rhyme for social satire echoes from beginning to end. The titles, the universalising closures, buoyant consolations and verbal extravagances can be off-putting unless they are understood to be, as they usually are, self-reflexive ironies.

Pitter's poems are ultimately rewarding for what Elizabeth Jennings, in her introduction, identifies as her "dedicated craftsmanship", her "skill with a variety of verse forms". The *Collected Poems* provide models for all kinds of structural antics and appropriations of traditional forms. For her clever blend of parody and pastiche see, for example, the spoof Elizabethan narrative 'The Earwig's Complaint – being the history of his doleful case miserably constrained to write ELEGY that would fain sing Epithalamion' or the mock-mediaeval blank verse, 'Timely Tydings for Loueles Ladyes'; 'Heroic Couplets' is a poor man's lament against the "very Englishman's" pomp and wealth, and the quasi-limerick 'Charity and its Object' a swipe at the self-

righteous do-gooder. There are numerous voices in the poetry and the tone is not always satirical. 'The Stolen Babe' is a gruesome Hardyesque monologue of a child murderer, and there are hymns, lyrical pastorals and elegies, a sonnet for Milton's Tercentenary, 1974, 'Valediction', and a two sentence experimental sonnet on bereavement, 'As when the faithful'.

To the late twentieth century reader, Ruth Pitter's contextualised observations like 'Cricket Match, 1908', 'Piblett, 1910' (the self-satisfied Edwardian gent.), or 'The Great Winter 1946-1947' will be most appealing, along with her unsettling portraits of untold tragedy such as 'Old, Childless, Husbandless' or 'The Solitary'; these achieve her intention of combining the "spirit of comedy" with "pain, illimitable anguish, horror and ennui".

Occasional Skeletons

by Paula Burnett

OLIVE SENIOR

Gardening in the Tropics

Bloodaxe, £7.95
ISBN 1 85224 293 0

BERNARDINE EVARISTO

Island of Abraham

Peepal Tree Books, £5.95
ISBN 0 948833 60 2

TO BE BLACK and a woman is hardly the easiest of primrose paths, but to *write* as a black woman today is to pick your way over a minefield. Gone is the (allegedly) easy claim to status, of speaking for those most silenced by history and by patriarchy, of having the authority (supposedly) to buttonhole the world with righteous indignation. The politics of writing has moved on, a reactionary rearguard only too ready to swing back into the van. Many well-known names, mostly American, enable the backlash to claim the task as done (as if writing can ever be "done"). In reality, experiences continue, vary, coalesce, diversify. Here a Jamaican now based

in Canada and a British woman with a Nigerian father write from the particularity of their perceptions – Senior making a welcome return to poetry after acquiring a fine reputation with prose fiction – but they both address, among other things, the black story, ongoing amidst a global politics of inequality. In Senior's collection the stoical survivors of natural cataclysms like hurricanes point the way to surviving man-made social disasters, while Evaristo in a memorable phrase says "I am not safe anywhere but learn / to discard fear like rotten fruit".

Some of Senior's poems are voiced by a distinctive Caribbean persona (though rarely using a markedly Jamaican English), addressing an implied reader who is white and of the privileged north. In the title sequence she evokes the tone of an ageing cultivator coaxing flourishing fruit, vegetables and flowers out of tropical soil – and the old-fashioned firmness and independence which go hand in gardening-glove with it: pride is the order of the day, and well-merited. Senior builds her collection around what might have been a tired equation of woman with regenerative nature, but makes it come across with the dew on it still. Like her persona, she knows she has something to teach the world. The rich north does not hold all the answers, far from it, as she reminds us, but is responsible for some of the worst horrors.

She is based in Toronto, but was in Britain in 1992 on an Arts Council award, and records here, among other things, her south-coast experience – putting spring flowers on Jean Rhys's Devon grave, for example, and pondering the sacrifices made by pioneers. In her eloquent 'Meditation on Red' Senior pays tribute: "I'll / be able to / find my way / home again / / for that craft / you launched / is so seaworthy / tighter / than you'd ever been / / dark voyagers / like me / can feel free / to sail". Speaking about her position as a writer at a recent conference in Milan, Senior said, "I feel that I'm occupying a space that has no defined boundaries".

The island of Abraham of Evaristo's title is Madagascar, symbolic isle of origin, place apart, paradise, but in reality a third world country in hock to neo-colonialism. The package is familiar perhaps, particularly from Caribbean literature, but Evaristo is a poet raised and resident in Britain who casts a different net over the terrain. In Madagascar she visits her father's continent. In her long focal poem, as an insider /outsider tourist she is targeted by begging children, and we get a glimpse of a French neo-colonial setting unfamiliar in English. The island plays a special role in imaginings of Africa, and in the 1940s inspired Mannoni's ground-breaking study of the psychology of colonialism, *Prospero and Caliban*, a psychology which Senior addresses from a fresh angle: the colonised person realises with surprise that "I unsettled you", the coloniser, "for you saw me / out there as your own unguarded / self, running free".

Olive Senior

Bently Quast

Both poets write specifically out of a female self. Senior images epic ancestors, "strong Amazon / women striding across our lands", but also a father whose banana plantation was turned a symbolic blue – from a chemical spray which produced blue leaves in which the banana bunches were wrapped for export. Deftly she tackles twin targets: the packaging of one culture by another, and the "blues" of third world realities, psychologically as well as materially crippling, particularly perhaps to men. In a new mythography she traces the Amazon myth to the women left behind by their men to fend for themselves. In the repeated migrations of history, "All, all the men went with our dreams, // our hopes, our prayers". In another poem a narrator overhears a woman warn her man, "With your

sweet words, Lover, tempt me / not, if you've come empty-handed". The oblique narration cools the temper without reducing the reach of the thought.

Like Senior, Evaristo looks past the patriarch suggested in her title to an ancestry of heroic women, but is still preoccupied with the father whose eyes she cannot fathom, who passed on his "inheritance of / principles, struggle and story / to be unravelled like gossamer". The book is dedicated, however, to her grandmother and includes a poem in her name: "Our thin bodies knelt in homage / as Zenobia strode towards us / from the foothills. / / Finely coiled hennaed hair / dancing about her thighs. / / Clenched teeth of cowrie shells / draped from her noble neck". The self-conscious claiming of such images is sometimes strained, but at other moments a phrase springs to life against the grain: as when African singing reminds her of a Welsh choir, rather than vice versa.

It is to Senior, however, that the reader who likes the light, ironic touch of Caribbean "picong" should turn. She has the control to follow an apocalyptic image, of volcanoes erupting skulls, with "Mine is only / a kitchen garden so I unearth just / occasional skeletons". She manages to be serious without being heavy, making skilful use of deceptively low-key voices. Just when you are settling pleasurably into a poem spoken by an elderly matron gossiping about family over her yard fence, Senior reveals the whole thing to be an allegory for Caribbean/US power relations, but without ruffling the surface tone of the poem. The effect is both exhilarating and disturbing, reminding us of how easy it is to live at that superficial level, oblivious to the real power-drama which props up our privileges.

At her best Evaristo displays a relaxed narrative talent and a moving lyricism, but the energy rising at the heart of her poems is too often dissipated in weak endings. Senior, the more experienced writer, has a surer touch. It is difficult to address a painful history without hysteria – to tease the wit out of witness – but the poems in these collections, which measure personal history against the collective story reaching back into myth, most reduce us to tears with a studied lack of histrionics.

The Home Front

by Elizabeth Lowry

RITA ANN HIGGINS

Sunny Side Plucked

Bloodaxe, £8.95

ISBN 1 85224 375 9

PAULA MEEHAN

Mysteries of the Home

Bloodaxe, £7.95

ISBN 1 85224 374 0

WHATEVER THEIR FINAL preference, Rita Ann Higgins's and Paula Meehan's fans should be pleased by Bloodaxe's decision to bring out the selected poems of these two popular Irish poets simultaneously. Side by side, their complementary approaches are thrown into even sharper relief: while Paula Meehan is sophisticated and allusive, Rita Ann Higgins goes in for plain speaking; where Meehan takes considered detours into academe, Higgins doesn't give a damn. For the reader with a ten pound note to spend, choosing between them will largely be a matter of taste.

Higgins's poems are really anecdotes – it's not how she tells them, so much as *what* she tells that matters, although the absence of an obvious technique can sometimes be a happy effect in her work. *Sunny Side Plucked* contains a generous sample of her signature sketches of urban Irish working-class types: young mothers on welfare, lottery players, blanket men and coal men, charity cases for the Vincent de Paul society, butter voucher and coupon savers. These are rounded out here and there into gritty character studies, the best of which stick in the mind because of the unfussy way they are presented – bored Evangeline pining on her way to Folan's shop for "a villa / off the something / coast of France" ('Evangeline'); tarty Karen Reilly who is shot in the back while driving a stolen car down the Falls Road ('The Trouble with Karen Reilly'); restless Philomena, whose rages are cured after she is given "the shocks" ('Philomena's Revenge'), and 'Tommy's Wife', bleakly anonymous, slowly drained by her marriage to Tommy (who "likes Guinness, sex and unemployment"). Galway-born Higgins knows this world, its aspirations and frus-

trations, and is able to capture its detail and its voice. The particulars of her backdrop – net curtains, leather jackets, home perms, the Saturday night dance, Chesterfield sofas and phone tables bought on hire-purchase – are filled in with economy, establishing a minimalist setting for brisk dramatic monologues with suitably colloquial-sounding titles such as 'Anything is Better than Emptying Bins', 'It's All Because We're Working-Class' and 'It Wasn't the Father's Fault'. At its most successful the transparency of Higgins's vision contributes to a flatness of expression which gives its own depressing point to the material. 'It Wasn't the Father's Fault', for instance, is an impassively nasty little story about a child whose father beat him up with a baseball bat, with the result that "he was / never right since":

Standing
behind the kitchen table
one Sunday before Mass
his mother said,

"If Birdie Geary
hadn't brought
that cursed baseball bat
over from America,

none of this would have happened".

The bathos of that last remark, in which natural feeling hasn't so much been suppressed as steamrollered out of shape, suggests emotional depletion with greater immediacy than a stanza of commentary could have at this point. Higgins's characters queue for the dole, save up those vouchers, and everyone keeps on going to Mass; but the missed connections are also heartbreakingly in the air in 'The Deserter', narrated by a woman whose unsatisfactory marriage has been given an injection of tenderness by the death of her husband ("he made a lovely corpse"), the prosy advice of 'If You Want to get Closer to God' ("Knock Shrine's your man ... plenty of wheelchairs / plenty of buses"), and the drab promises of Consumpta the hairdresser in 'I Want to Make Love to Kim Basinger' ("hot oil / is the jigger you need ... you'll taste your tea then / and it won't be wearing a moustache, / mark my words"). Promises, platitudes. Where Higgins herself appears as a character alongside the Karens and Consumptas, her poetic ambitions are treated with appealing self-mockery. An afternoon spent trying to learn her trade in the reference room of the Galway County Library is scuppered by a bowsy with a cough who has settled on the poetry section as a change of scene from the local soup kitchen. Here the banal keeps breaking in, rather as it does in the poems themselves:

> I started with Heaney,
> you started to cough.
> You coughed all the way to Ormsby,
> I was on the verge of Mahon.
>
> Daunted, I left you the Ulster Poets
> to consume or cough at.

In fact, Higgins is consistently self-deprecating about her bookishness. The odd literary or classical theme is ruthlessly cut down to size by being relayed in Irish slang – her Donna Laura calls Petrarch a "louser", Hera refers to Zeus as "loveen", and 'The Flute Girl's Dialogue', a downmarket version of the *Symposium*, begins with the freewheeling lines "Plato, come out now / with your sunburnt legs on ya". 'The Quarrel', in which the story of the Trojan war is transplanted to a Shantalla tenement, has Apollo practising the lyre, "mad to get / on *The Late Late Show*", while Zeus's activities – in the vicinity of Coole Park, presumably – make "swans all over Sligo" take "cover, much cover". Yeats must be turning in his grave.

Paula Meehan

If Higgins shores up her fragments, Paula Meehan goes in for the grand synthesis. *Mysteries of the Home* is a *Bildungsroman* of sorts, complete with prologue and epilogue. The book's dramatically staggered sequences – and the intimate tone of Meehan's poetry suggests that the story told here is her own – re-enact the end of a marriage, followed by travel, a difficult emotional recovery and gradual rebirth. A courageous and searching analysis of her own hereditary weaknesses and strengths runs parallel to this surface narrative. 'The Pattern', one of several poems in which Meehan remembers her early years in Dublin, describes her mother buffing the floors of their small flat, defeated by domesticity. It also indicates what the challenge to the child will be:

> Tongues of flame in her dark eyes,
> she'd say, "One of these days I must
> teach you to follow a pattern".

Although in memory the city of Meehan's childhood has become a stygian place, "a chilled vault / littered with totems", the volume's most lyrical visual passages belong to her recollections of this period and setting. Rapt recreations of a late-night journey home carrying newspaper twists of winkles "like torches" ('Buying Winkles'), or a stroll through the Natural History Museum, "found poem / of oriole, kingfisher, sparrowhawk, nightjar" ('A Child's Map of Dublin'), hint at an ambiguity of response that is also there in the account of her later, unsuccessful marriage. In 'Zugzwang' she is settled in suburban comfort in a Vermeer-like interior, except that the snug room is suddenly bathed in a polar light as Meehan, apparently reconciled to domesticity as her mother was before her, begins to hear the latter's voice repeating, "*I told you so, I told you so, I told you so*". What happens next is represented obliquely, through the shamanistic imagery of myth. 'Full Moon' and 'On the Warpath' establish an identification with the moon goddess of Irish folklore, reinforced with allusions to shapechanging and the cyclical disruptions of menstruation. Newly empowered as priestess of the rites, the atavistic female consciousness ("speaker" would be too feeble a word) of the later poems sacrifices her marriage, takes a lover and escapes from cosy suburbia. As if submitting to the pressure of her theme, Meehan's language takes on a hieratic formality – there are stilted references to "the signals of my garb" ('On Being Taken for a Turkish Woman'), the shadows of clouds "oblivious of the grief on our faces" ('Not alone the rue in my herb garden . . .') and the shaking "asunder" of a mind and heart ('The Man who was Marked by Winter'). This is occasionally combined with that other hieratic language, the language of psychotherapy, as she tries to uncover the origins of her original impasse. Unsurprisingly, perhaps, 'The Wounded Child' (the title of which reads a little too much as if it were supplied by Alice Miller) locates her tragedy in the example set by her mother. The diagnosis is convincing enough, if only the solution weren't stated quite as reductively as this: "Rescue the child / from her dark spell! / Rescue the child / from her dark spell! / Rescue the child".

The book's final poem, 'Home', fatalistically implies that the pattern of conformity was already laid down in the womb where, while attached to the umbilicus, "I was a pitiful monkey jigging on cue". In the end, however, Meehan decides not to press charges. The envoi, 'Seed', shows her making up her mind, Candide-like, to cultivate her garden instead, trusting to "the power of seed, / its casual, useful persistence". It's a sane gesture from a candid poet who will, no doubt, coax this hard-won self knowledge to full fruition in her next volume.

NEWS/COMMENT

A TALE OF TWO ANTHOLOGIES

To celebrate his ten years at the *Literary Review* Auberon Waugh has issued the third anthology of poetry that rhymes, scans and makes sense taken from the magazine's competition: *It's Her Voice that Haunts Me Now* (edited by Dariane Pictet and published by Richard Cohen Books, £8.99, ISBN 1 86066 092 4). Waugh's introduction jeers at the Poetry Olympics held at the Albert Hall in July '96, which he seems to think was organised by the Poetry Society (cue for more jeers about State-funded poetry) – the event was, of course, entirely Michael Horovitz's responsibility. He also thinks that the performers were "the usual handful of more or less untalented exibitionists who are the official voice of poetry in out time". The bill (commemorated in *The POW! Anthology*, New Departures, PO Box 9819, London W11 2GQ, £6.99 (£7.99 inc p&p), ISBN 0 902689 17 7) was in fact a typically idiosyncratic Horovitz menu, with a few more mainstream poets than usual – James Fenton, Carol Ann Duffy, Paul Durcan, Simon Armitage, Miroslav Holub, Sujata Bhatt, Gwyneth Lewis – mixing it with pop stars (Patti Smith, Damon Albarn, Kylie Minogue and Ray Davies and old Horovitz favourites like Ifigenija Simonovic, Heathcote Williams, Inge Elsa Laird.

The *Literary Review*'s selection consists of garlands of Georgian light verse on set themes: 'A Threnody for Tobacco' ("O! But it was a lovely, lovely thing / To slip aside the outer packaging ..."); 'Lessons' ("See the wide-eyed piccaninny . . ."); 'An English Heaven' ("Hello, hello, it's Mum, my dears, / So cheer up now and dry those tears ...").

The POW! Anthology is a "a spontaneous bop collection rattled together over a weekend" (translation: you can't knock the production standards). It is an endearingly dotty mix. Some of these people could never appear between the same covers unless it were Horovitz orchestrating them: Fran Landesmann is a great songwriter ('Spring can really hang you up the most') represented here by the cute 'I Quite Like Men', which might at a pinch have made it into *It's Her Voice*. There are classics from the likes of Fenton ('The Mistake'), Kit Wright ('I Found South African Breweries most Hospitable') plus a fair helping of woozy Horovitziana – a Damon Albarn worksheet, a Jah Wobble poem printed in caps, a few hand-written poems – but in the end you have to warm to something so exuberantly polymorphous: from E. J. Thribb's 'In Memoriam Dr Timothy Leary ("Personally I / think Keith / has dropped / too much / acid / / M-a-a-a-n"), through Grace Nichols, Hanif Kureishi, John Cooper Clark, to Miroslav Holub. Let's hope Bron had one for Christmas.

NET VERSE

Regular readers will know that there's a plethora of Websites hosting new poetry, electronic magazines, or archives of established poetry. What I haven't mentioned is the emergence of hypertext poetry, which the Web hasn't exactly invented, but has made much more widely available. Hypertext is the concept of clicking on highlighted words to bring up other, related text; hypertext poetry is where the text in question is a poem. One of the gurus of the form is Robert Kendall whose own page at **http://ourworld.compuserve.com/homepages/ rkendall/** contains a good introduction to the genre. More information can be found at **http://ebbs. english.vt.edu/** or **http://www.academic.marist. edu/culture.htm**

Eastgate Systems, at **http://www.eastgate.com/** is a commercial outfit producing software for generating hypertext. Their site always has examples, and you can subscribe to their (free) e-mail newsletter which has news of hypertext projects (and plugs for their software, of course).

So much for theory: what about the practice? One simple possibility is to provide pointers to background material, as is done with Carroll's *Jabberwocky* at **http://sar.usf.edu/~zazuetaa/ jabberwocky/start.html**. More innovative are efforts to make hypertext an intrinsic element of the poetry, such as the linked poems at **http://www.sund.ac.uk/~us0cma/europa.html** and the epigrammatic verse at **http://camel. conncoll.edu/ccother/wjbat/Sense_cov.html**

Jim Rosenberg at **http://www.well.com/user/ jer/** uses a somewhat different technique he calls "intergrams" which is probably pushing the current technology. I'm not sure if the meditative Chinese stuff at **http://www.aloha.com/~craven/dovered. html** really counts as hypertext poetry, but it's certainly different.

You can find more links to hypertext theory, and examples of it, in Tom Beard's Library, **http :// www.met.co.nz/nwfc/beard/www/Library. html**

Regular readers will also know that I don't think

much of usenet newsgroups. That bit of copy (from *PR* 86/2) found its way onto the **rec.arts.poems** group, but I didn't get flamed, worse luck. But Douglas Clark takes me to task for saying he's English, rather than British. Sorry, Douglas. Other complaints to **peter@hphoward.demon.co.uk**

PETER HOWARD

The Poetry Society's website can now be found at: **http://www.bbc.co.uk/poetry_soc/**

INVITATION: IMAGINED POETS AND HOAXES

From Ossian, through Ern Malley, to Jason Strugnell and E. J. Thribb – these were the poets who, because they didn't exist, had to be invented. For a future issue, we are seeking further examples of poetic hoaxes and synthetic poets. They can be single poems fobbed off on editors or entire Malley-like *oeuvres*. We'd also be glad to hear from anyone who has a particular interest in and knowledge of any of the poets named at the head of this paragraph. Deadline: March 1st.

COMPETITION

REPORT ON NO 3: TENSE FODDER

You were asked for resonant titles for avant-garde magazines or pamphlets.

"The essential titles are: *P=A=T=O=I=S=E=R=I=E, Smegma Cull, Grindstone Alert, Deadsea Scrawls,* but *Primal Squeak* also looks significant".

– Bill Turner

NO 4: OUR IAN

Ian McMillan thinks Susan Wicks writes in a "special three dimensional ink the rest of us are denied access to" (that one made Pseuds Corner) and that Maura Dooley's technique can best be compared to that Eric Morecambe. Clearly reviewers have been too timid in their search for the roots of a poet's art. Creative contexts, similes, and metaphors for the Ian's own practice wanted. Deadline: Feb 25th. Prize: A handful of books, including Eliot's juvenilia, Paulin's essays, the new Redgrove and Murray, Auden's *As I Walked Out One Evening.*

LETTERS

OBJECT LESSONS

Dear Editor,

If I thought a poet cloth-eared, clumsy and obscure, I wouldn't rush to defend her, whatever her other qualities. In fact, unlike Ms. Jamie, I didn't say any of that about Eavan Boland. I said that though I admired her skill, she was not to my taste. Has Jamie never encountered writers whose quality she can recognise, but not respond to – who, for all their skill, leave her cold because of something in their themes, stances, style? Well, Boland does that to me, and provided I acknowledge that it's *my* response I don't see the harm in admitting it. I feel no obligation to empathise more with her work because we're both women, or both Celts, least of all because she's a PBS choice. I wouldn't dream of letting the PBS make up my mind for me. Whoever else likes a poet, reviewers should judge for themselves, and much as I differ from John Hartley Williams, I do admire him for having the guts to go against the crowd – the only thing that worries me about my own Doty-worship is the scary sense of being in a majority for once!

I did warn the editor that I was lukewarm about Boland, so that he could, if he wished, choose another reviewer. He didn't, so perhaps he felt that the main job of a review was not, actually, to provide an in-depth analysis of a poet's work to date. If you want that, you hire someone to write a critical article on them. In a review you try, within strict word limits, to give general poetry readers (who may not be, or want to become, experts on any particular poet) some idea of what a book's like and whether they're liable to enjoy it – which I didn't; so was it not legitimate to say so?

Regards,
SHEENAGH PUGH
Cardiff

SERMONS IN STONES

Dear Peter,

All words are metaphors.

Yours sincerely,
JENNY JOSEPH
Minchinhampton,
Glos.

SOME CONTRIBUTORS

Smita Agarwal won 2nd Prize in the 1994 British Council/Poetry Society of India All-India Poetry Competition.
Gillian Allnutt's new collection, *Nantucket and the Angel*, is forthcoming from Bloodaxe.
Moniza Alvi's latest collection is *Warm Air* (Oxford Poets, 1996).
Annemarie Austin's latest collection is *The Flaying of Marsyas* (Bloodaxe, 1995).
Elizabeth Bartlett's *Selected Poems: Two Women Dancing* was published by Bloodaxe in 1995.
Connie Bensley's *Central Reservations: New & Selected Poems* was published by Bloodaxe in 1990.
Paula Burnett is editor of *The Penguin Book of Caribbean Poetry*.
Jane Dowson has edited Frances Cornford's *Selected Poems* (Enitharmon, 1996).
Carol Ann Duffy's *Selected Poems* are published by Penguin.
U. A. Fanthorpe's *Safe as Houses* (Peterloo) is shortlisted for the Whitbread Award.
Elaine Feinstein's *Selected Poems* were published by Carcanet in 1995.
Linda France is the editor of *Sixty Women Poets* (Bloodaxe, 1993).
Elizabeth Garrett's first collection, *The Rule of Three*, was published by Bloodaxe in 1991.
John Greening's latest collections are *The Coastal Path* (Headland) and *The Bocase Stone* (Dedalus).
Atar Hadari was a featured new poet in *PR*, Vol 86 No 1.
Jenny Joseph's 'Warning' is the Nation's Favourite Poem.
Jackie Kay's latest collection is *Other Lovers* (Bloodaxe, 1993).
James Keery's first collection, *That Stranger, The Blues*, was published in 1996 by Carcanet.
Hermione Lee's biography of *Virginia Woolf* was published by Chatto in 1996.
Ian McMillan's latest collection is *Dad, the Donkey's On Fire* (Carcanet, 1995).
Medbh McGuckian's latest collection is *Captain Lavender* (Gallery, 1995).
Dennis O'Driscoll's new collection, *Quality Time*, is due from Anvil in the Spring.
Maggie O'Farrell works on the Arts and Books pages of the *Independent on Sunday*.
Carol Rumens' latest collection is *Best China Sky* (Bloodaxe).
Eva Salzman's new collection, *Bargain with the Watchman*, is due from Oxford Poets in May.
Carole Satyamurti's latest collection is *Striking Distance* (Oxford Poets, 1994).
Jo Shapcott is co-editor (with Matthew Sweeney) of *Emergency Kit* (Faber).
Adam Thorpe's third novel and third book of poems are forthcoming from Cape.
Susan Wicks' new collection is forthcoming from Faber.
John Hartley Williams' memoir, *Ignoble Sentiments*, is published by Arc.

ERRATA

Volume 86 No 3, Autumn 1996, p.71: Kamau Brathwaite's poem 'Wings of a Dove' was reprinted from *The Arrivants* (1973) by permission of Oxford University Press.
p.79: Helen Kidd is a contributor to, not the author of, *Calemadonnas, Women and Scotland* (Gairfish, 1994).